Roam Alone

INSPIRING TALES
BY RELUCTANT
SOLO TRAVELLERS

Compiled and edited by
Jennifer Barclay and Hilary Bradt

First published in the UK in April 2017 by

Bradt Travel Guides Ltd
IDC House, The Vale, Chalfont St Peter, Bucks SL9 9RZ, England
www.bradtguides.com

Print edition published in the USA by The Globe Pequot Press Inc,
PO Box 480, Guilford, Connecticut 06437-0480

Text copyright © 2017 Bradt Travel Guides Ltd
Chapter introductions by Hilary Bradt
Edited by Jennifer Barclay and Hilary Bradt
Copy-edited by Ian Robert Smith
Proofread by Janet Mears
Cover design: illustration and concept by Neil Gower, typesetting by Ian Spick
Typesetting and digital conversion by www.dataworks.co.in
Production managed by Sue Cooper and Jellyfish Print Solutions
Printed in the UK

ISBN: 978 1 78477 049 5 (print)
e-ISBN: 978 1 78477 507 0 (e-pub)
e-ISBN: 978 1 78477 408 0 (mobi)

British Library Cataloguing in Publication Data
A catalogue record for this book is available from the British Library

Contents

Foreword

Jan Leeming

I first encountered Bradt's colourful series of true-life travel tales when I was presented with a copy of *To Oldly Go: Tales of Intrepid Travel by the Over-60s* and made the innocent mistake of taking it on a train journey. As I read its stories, I burst out laughing until I cried, receiving hard stares from all around me. It was therefore a great pleasure to have the opportunity to write a foreword to *Roam Alone: Inspiring Tales by Reluctant Solo Travellers*. This superb collection has given me hours of enjoyment as I experience with the writers the highs and lows, delights and tribulations of single travel all over the world.

When I worked in the stressful environment of television, my idea of a holiday was chilling out on a lovely beach with some good historical novels – and, until fourteen years ago, I was fortunate enough to be able to share those times with a companion. As I got older, though, I wanted fuller experiences from my travels.

I'm no shrinking violet and have done some relatively adventurous activities: wing-walking for charity, for instance, and flying in display with the Red Arrows and The Blades Aerobatic Team (all ex-Reds). I even accepted a place on *I'm a Celebrity... Get Me Out of Here!* on the say so of my son. 'Go on, mother,' he said, 'you'll be first out and can enjoy a two-week holiday in a six-star hotel at

Surfers Paradise.' Fat chance! I was voted on to six trials, and had to endure being 'thrown' out of a plane at fourteen thousand feet on a buddy jump, being placed in a perspex box with a dozen varieties of snake, and being dropped into a dark 'mineshaft' where I had to put my hands into holes containing unmentionables! (Thank you, my son.) I've travelled the outback in New South Wales; slept in an ice hotel at minus five degrees; broken down at night on a skimobile on a frozen lake in Norway; and learned to ski at the age of sixty-two.

Yet in spite of this, I lacked the courage to travel alone apart from visiting relations and friends in Australia and France. I hadn't had an 'adventure' for over a decade; where solo travel was concerned, my get-up-and-go had got up and gone.

Then, like the answer to a prayer, I came across Just You Singles Holidays – one of several companies that specialise in holidays for solo travellers. So I packed my case and went off to Myanmar with a group. It was a voyage of discovery and we hardly drew breath, experiencing so much of Burmese culture in eleven days. We lunched with Buddhist nuns, visited mountain villages, watched craftspeople from weavers to gold workers, flew across Inle Lake in huge 'speedboats' and took off our shoes at so many temples I wondered if it was worth the bother of wearing them at all. If there was any problem, the tour manager absorbed it and we never had to carry luggage – another difficulty as we age. I wish I'd been more adventurous when younger – but thank goodness it's not too late.

I've loved the stories in *Roam Alone*, which moved me to tears of both sadness and joy. Ian Douglas's 'A Coconut with Three Candles' was one of the former, an emotional account of backpacking to Chiang Mai with Kobra, a one-handed young guide whose job meant the difference between life and starvation.

By contrast, Phoebe Smith's 'Not so Solo at Sea' made me laugh – so much of me was there in her reservations about sharing a cabin with a total stranger, an experience which actually worked out so well that when she finally got her luxury night in a hotel in Ushuaia she missed having someone with whom to share the day's events.

Every aspect of single travel features in *Roam Alone* and there are useful tips from Silver Travel Advisor and other experts too. Many of the contributors are award-winning writers and their ability shines through, transforming what could be ordinary tales into literary gems. Although the emphasis is obviously on travel, I would highly recommend this delightful book to anyone who likes short stories. It is an ideal book to take on a train, plane or boat journey – or to read from the comfort of an armchair, vicariously enjoying the world and hopefully finding the inspiration to try travelling solo yourself.

And if you have got wanderlust or the courage to 'go it alone', with over two hundred titles from which to choose, Bradt's published world is your oyster.

Introduction
Hilary Bradt

I've spent so long pretending I'm fine about travelling alone that I've almost forgotten I'm not. I'd much prefer a like-minded companion. But then I look back on all those trips where I had to go solo, back to the sheer exhilaration of the best moments, and I think what an added richness it's given my travel memories and how fortunate I am to have been forced to do it when companions dropped out. Because this is how it usually happens. As you'll see from the stories in this book, the reluctant solo traveller generally doesn't plan to travel alone; it's just that the desire to travel is stronger than the fear. Thank God.

We have this idea that celebrity travellers are never afraid. It doesn't gel with the intrepid image, and is anyway something that they have to deal with unobtrusively. But I bet a lot of them share our nervousness. Hannah Stuart-Leach, one of the most fearful (and therefore the bravest) contributors to this book, sums it up for all of us: 'The only way I've found to combat anxiety is, as self-help gurus so carelessly advise, to feel the fear and do it anyway.' And that's what all the story-tellers here have done. They have all been reluctant travellers, they have all kept to their plans despite their doubts and they have all profited from their courage. Many have become more confident in their everyday lives after returning home.

There are, of course, numerous travellers who choose to go solo, with never a twinge of anxiety, because they know the advantages. And there are so many advantages over travelling in couples or groups. Perhaps the biggest plus, which comes out in many of these stories, is that solo travellers meet the locals. They have to. And once the initial unease has worn off, they want to. Many are invited into homes and quickly become immersed in the culture. They also have the opportunity to link up with other travellers (and most of us, whether sneakily or openly, do want to speak our own language and share common experiences from time to time during our travels). There are stories of these brief or lasting friendships as well. But to some, that dreaded trip has become a life-changer, putting the traveller on a new career that was undreamt of when they queued at check-in, their heart pounding at the audacity of what they were setting out to do.

If we can do it, anyone can. Be inspired!

The First Step

⊕ ⊕ ⊕

Taking the plunge to travel solo for the first time is not easy. These writers examine the courage it took and the rewarding experiences that were the result. Sandra Reekie sets out in her mid-fifties to travel solo in India, despite never having travelled alone. 'When we went abroad on holiday I had never even used the foreign currency – I was petrified.' An impulsive decision to accept a volunteer placement at Camp America turns another hesitant newbie into a seasoned solo traveller, and a trip to Gabon could so easily not have happened '... with the ease of not going outweighing my desire to go'. Amanda Lumley nearly missed her flight to Australia because of her reluctance to take the first step by boarding the Tube to the airport, and Kirsty Fergusson barely has the money for an InterRail card but her longing to escape leads to some extraordinary meetings.

Really? On My Own?

Sandra Reekie

'You will never see a sky as beautiful as the sun rising over the Himalayas from Darjeeling,' my father said with an unaccustomed hint of nostalgia in his voice. I was four or five years old and we were sitting atop a hill watching the sun go down over the Essex town where we lived. From that moment, that exact moment, I longed to see that sunrise for myself and visit Agra where my grandfather was stationed with the British Army when Dad was born.

But it took me a while. Fifty years later, my daughter and I travelled independently to India, and we did indeed see that sunrise and Agra. A nine-week trip with my daughter made me realise that it was possible to find your own hotels, discover what's down that small and interesting-looking road the tour guide walks you past and, most importantly of all, learn just how incredibly friendly and kind people are to a stranger. The travel bug had bitten, and bitten hard.

The following year I had a close call with cancer and when I didn't die within the predicted year, I resolved to go back to India. No-one would or could come with me so, pig-headedly, I said I'd go on my own. It was an easy thing to say, but could I really go alone? Really *on my own*? After I'd said goodbye to my husband at Heathrow, I went into the ladies and sobbed. What was I doing?

I had never travelled on my own. When we went abroad on holiday I had never even used the foreign currency – I was petrified. So I had cheated a little and booked the first ten days with a small group adventure travel company to help me get over my initial nerves. We spent those first ten days travelling to Kochi, Mysore and Ootacamund; then I said goodbye and headed alone for the railway station in Bangalore to catch the overnight train to Hampi.

This fascinating historical site, set in a strange and beautiful, boulder-strewn landscape, was in fact the perfect place for me to explore for the first time completely on my own. Each day my confidence grew and with it my sense of awareness and safety. What was I doing? Was it respectful? A deserted restaurant was probably not as safe as a full one. I learned to trust my gut feeling when it came to judging people. I found that all these long-buried skills, which we all possess, were slowly getting stronger. And before I left there, I'd even found myself part of a Bollywood movie.

I needed to travel north, but I wanted to see Panaji, the capital of Goa, and for the first time caught an overnight bus. Imagine if you will a double decker painted bright yellow, with homemade reclining seats. I was allocated a window seat which reclined so far back my feet were above my head and the lever was broken. Next to me sat an enormous bald German man whose bulk spread from his recliner on to mine. As we rattled our way along the bumpy Indian roads in the pitch black, any 'comfort' stops were made at the side of the road and each time at least one person came back with cuts and grazes, having fallen down a ditch. But we made it to Goa. Those who had the top deck fared best, as most were enjoying some 'happy baccy', but I had a new German friend.

From Goa I found my way by bus, train, taxi and rickshaw to the ancient caves at Ellora and also to those at Ajanta. At the Ajanta Caves I was adopted by a taxi driver who decided that, as I was older than his mother, I needed looking after. I suspiciously thought he just wanted to overcharge me for each ride, but how wrong I was. It was another lesson learned – to trust my own judgement and not go by the alarmist stories you hear.

I was so proud of myself. I had not only achieved my first trip alone, but I had managed all my travel arrangements, even come to grips with the bureaucratic purchasing of train tickets and finally, with just two days before my return flight, made it to Mumbai arriving in the early hours at that wonderful carved stone-and-marble railway station six weeks after setting out. Boy, did I feel good!

I subsequently returned to India on several occasions, sometimes alone, sometimes not. I also travelled along the Silk Road – starting in Istanbul, I crossed Turkey, Syria, Iran and Turkmenistan with its bizarre capital, Ashgabat. Then I travelled on to Uzbekistan, Tajikistan and China where I visited the largest Silk Road market in the world at Kashgar, before crossing into Pakistan at the highest paved border crossing in the world.

I made friends along the way; many are still Facebook friends. Sometimes I joined up with people who were going my way for a few days or a week or two, such as the young man with whom I shared the hire of a car to cross the Pamir Mountains. I have wonderful memories of many people – the kindly Sikh man who, without my knowing, kept his eye on me during a three-hour wait at an Indian railway station and who, when I nearly boarded the wrong train, gently took my arm and shook his head; the lady on a long bus journey in Iran who planted a large bag of sweets on my lap; and the student in Syria who waited twenty minutes with me to ensure I caught the right bus and the driver knew where to let me off. I have a well of such memories.

In northern Pakistan I met a young Jeep driver. The following year I returned to live with his large extended family for a month, teaching at the local school, before taking two months to travel through every valley between Afghanistan and Kashmir in the Northern Areas of Pakistan. In one village I was the first foreign woman anyone could remember ever seeing.

We all know the old sayings like, 'Life isn't a rehearsal,' and looking back over my life I now realise that whenever I made myself do something that scared me, it always turned out to be the best experience ever. Travelling alone is one. I can't deny it can be lonely sometimes, but travelling with the wrong person is far, far worse. After years of being a daughter, wife, mother and grannie, I am now *me*. I love to travel with the right person, but if they aren't going my way I know I can happily go on my own.

At seventy-three, I must confess that it's time to retire my beloved rucksack and get something on wheels, but so long as I have a good guidebook and a water heater to make a cup of coffee, there's nothing can stop me.

Sandra Reekie lives in London with her husband of fifty-two years, David. She has two daughters and six grandchildren, and as they live in Herefordshire and Canada she is not too involved with grannie duties, which allows her to travel and arrange trips for her U3A group. She loves keeping open house for the friends she makes when travelling and showing them round London. She is a keen member of the Globetrotters Club in London and gives travel advice at the Adventure Travel Show at Olympia.

Short Notice
Helen Brown

The bus lurched violently around a corner. I was thrown to one side and the seatbelt dug painfully into my shoulder and body. Stanley reached his hand out as his wheelchair tipped, grasping at air as he tried to grip the bar under the window. I shoved my foot into his chair, pushing it back upright. I was still spread in an awkward position when my phone rang, as the man in my care thrust his chin at his water bottle, wanting a drink but unable to ask. I was a care assistant for physically disabled people at a holiday centre in Nottingham (imagine Butlins with wheels), and taking care of thirty guests at a time wasn't new to me. I could multi-task.

I jammed the phone under my ear as I answered it, putting the straw from the bottle in Stanley's mouth at the same time.

'Hello? Yes, that's me...'

The lady on the phone sounded American, and seemed to be talking about the volunteer programme I'd applied for a while back. Camp America. I hadn't thought about it for months now. Stanley nodded at me and I tried to put the cap on the water bottle without dropping the phone. I was only half concentrating on the American lady as the bus went around another corner and I was thrown to one side again, spilling half the bottle's contents down my standard-issue navy polo shirt. Then I thought I heard her say something along the lines of a flight, and my attention picked up.

'I'm sorry, I'm at work. Can you repeat that?'

She sighed with what sounded like mild frustration, before answering me. 'We've had a last minute cancellation. The only problem is the flight is in two days' time. I'm afraid I will need an answer quickly so we can fill the place.'

'Erm...'

After a stunned silence and a couple of questions I said I'd get back to her, to which she said that I'd have to give her an answer when she rang me back in half an hour. If I didn't answer then she'd have to give the place to someone else.

My heart sank as soon as I put the phone down, as it does when you realise you've done something really stupid. I had been scared, I had hesitated. *I should have said yes... Of course I should have said yes.*

I picked up my phone to try and ring her back, my hands shaking. I pressed the call button, jabbing furiously. The screen flashed and went black, dying before my eyes in an act of revenge for my idiocy. Had I just thrown this away?

I figured I was only five minutes from work, but there were no chargers for my phone at work and no-one with the same phone as me. I'd have to get home before she rang.

I nervously fidgeted, mentally urging the driver to go faster. When we finally arrived, I tumbled off the bus and handed over to a colleague as I babbled about flights, phones, batteries and America.

I left her looking confused and slightly irritated as I legged it.

Two hours later I was home when I heard the key turn in the door. Charlie, my housemate, walked into the living room to find me sitting on the carpet. In front of me was an empty suitcase, three large piles of clothing constituting my entire wardrobe, and a glass of whisky. I was just staring at the suitcase in a state of semi-shock.

'What on earth are you doing?' she asked, raising an eyebrow in amusement.

I wasn't sure if she was referring to the whisky, the non-packing, or my answer to the American lady.

I shook my head at her in answer to everything. 'I genuinely have no idea.' And I didn't. About anything. I was terrified. I'd not been on a plane since I was about ten years old, and never further than Europe. What was I doing?

'But you're going?'

I looked at her and nodded. 'I'm going. In two days I'm going to Vermont.'

Charlie laughed. 'You'd better start packing then,' she said, starting to rifle through my floor-drobe.

Originally she'd meant to go with me. We'd planned it together months ago, but she'd pulled out for family reasons, and now I was going on my own. I hadn't thought for a second I would actually get a place. Not at this late stage especially, though a couple of months back I'd put myself on bank shifts at work rather than a full-time contract just in case. I finished my glass of whisky as Charlie started throwing clothes in my case.

Before I knew it, it was Sunday and I was drinking free whisky on a long-haul flight to New York. I couldn't quite believe it. And somehow I had to get to Vermont on my own. They'd told me how to do it, but I was literally terrified.

When I reached the infamous Port Authority Bus Terminal in New York City I realised that my person-sized fuchsia pink suitcase was ridiculous. It was like a glaringly obvious sign that I was a first-time solo traveller from another country, asking to be robbed.

My pulse raced as I tried to rush through the crowded bus station. I shoved my way through the random mix of passengers, travellers with grubby backpacks and locals who had what seemed to be their entire lives stuffed into large plastic shopping bags. I looked down at my feet as I squeezed past them, wanting more than anything to reach the safety of the bus.

But then I got to the bus. It was fairly old, dusty with dirty windows and a musty smell. The seats were faded and threadbare and the other passengers were varied and intimidating. It didn't feel that safe anymore. One passenger was a young lad wearing red shorts and a black top, with headphones blaring out too-loud hip hop music. He was smoking a cigarette outside the doors of the bus and just stared as I struggled to shove my case in the space for luggage.

Soon the bus was rumbling through the city of New York, which was still buzzing with life though it was now late. I looked through the dirty window in amazement as we passed the lights and sounds of a city still very much alive – people shopping and eating, homeless people begging on corners with cardboard signs, locals rushing into subway stations carrying coffee from Starbucks, yellow taxis speeding past. As we drove over the bridge and left the city behind I craned my neck to look back at the sparkling skyline receding behind us. It suddenly hit me. Two days ago I was taking part in the daily chaos of being a care assistant; now I was on a bus, by myself, in the United States of America looking at the New York City skyline. It was enough to take my breath away. This was travelling. This was seeing the world. This was the moment – on a grimy Greyhound bus, having been awake for hours, alone and scared in one of the busiest cities in the world – this was the moment I truly understood the word *wanderlust*.

That was seven years ago, and I know now that trip was the start of a lifelong passion, wakening something in my soul – an urge to see the world, to experience life in all its beautiful variations. That summer was truly the best of my life so far. After I had finished the twelve weeks of volunteering at camp I met other travellers and we planned a road trip together. It began fantastically when we accidentally drove across the border into Canada at Niagara Falls, when we got confused on the highway, and ended with an unforgettable four-day drive to California down the iconic Route 66. I then did some solo travelling before coming home. I have since travelled to various amazing places around the world, always solo, sometimes joining small group tours temporarily and sometimes going it completely alone. I've visited five continents and many countries, and am a well-seasoned traveller compared to my younger clueless self. If I hadn't taken that initial plunge none of this would have happened. My advice? Take a risk. Always. You won't regret it.

Helen Brown is now a pilot officer in the Royal Air Force, and travelling will be a central part of her future career. Writing is her other love, and she was a regular writer for a local free paper in her home town of Sheffield before joining the RAF.

Gabon Confidential
Ian Packham

A large pair of ears started to flap gently, either side of a fat grey boulder; a twisting trunk rose from the vegetation nearby. A second trunk appeared, checking out my scent, before both dropped back into the grass, seemingly unconcerned by my presence. I was lucky to see elephants. Gabon's forest elephants were much shyer than their savannah cousins in east Africa's national parks and still almost entirely unused to humans. It was the result, my guide told me, of the country's low tourist numbers and the animals' love of their dense forest home.

It was the desire to break the habit of a lifetime that made me take the plunge and visit Gabon, sometimes called the Costa Rica of Africa, despite having to travel there alone. Looking back, it could have been very different, with the ease of not going outweighing my desire to go. Holding off from making any sort of commitment, I hadn't requested any time off work; nor had I booked flights, organised a visa or allowed any needles to become intimately associated with my upper arms. Meanwhile time was running out to make it to Gabon that year before the end of the dry season's good weather.

In previous situations such as this, I had put the decision off until it was too late to do anything but give up the idea. Not being able to convince any of my friends to travel with me, despite assurances of interest in the pub, was close to being the final nail in the coffin for yet another pipedream of an adventure.

When I was growing up, my family were conservative travellers, taking advantage of cheap packages to get us not much further than the Austrian Alps or Italian lakes on holidays where everything was organised and nothing left to chance but the weather. No-one in my family had had the opportunity to become a child of the British Empire, with my nearest and dearest instead clinging resolutely to small-town Surrey and its good rail connections with London. I'd had opportunities, but that didn't take away the fear – not only fear of the unknown, but also of facing that unknown alone, without anyone with whom I might talk through problems, discuss things like meals and hotel rooms and share costs. Yet my dream of seeing Gabon's wildlife, and the desire to take a risk just this once, made me go for it. I booked a non-refundable airline ticket to Libreville.

Oddly enough, it was on arrival at the airport departure gate that I finally relaxed, after catching sight of a lady at least twice my age, wearing a khaki-coloured twin-set and a large string of pearls around her neck. About to board the same flight as me, as alone as I was, she displayed so much more exterior poise and elegance than I could ever muster. Internally, I liked to think that she was as anxious as I remained.

Though Libreville is the most chic, stylish and French of Africa's capitals – its pâtisseries producing the finest éclairs this far south of Marseille and its restaurants the most *à la mode* of cuisines – it was the people I warmed to. Travelling alone pushed me into connecting with the Gabonese to a much greater extent than I ever would have had to as part of a group, and for me that was the true joy of independent solo travel.

Amid the frenzy of the streets, hawkers swathed in colourful wax-cloth prints took pride in choosing their best pineapples for me, deftly welding machetes to slice the fruit into juicy mouth-sized chunks. Smiling broadly, they took pains to teach me the correct way to pronounce *riz*, while pouring the hottest of homemade chilli sauces on to the rice I had ordered from their roadside stalls. A nightclub owner, discovering that I was alone, invited me to dance the night away at a private party. And it was locals who stopped me in the shade of the coconut palms between the Presidential Palace and the National Museum and encouraged me to take the Trans-Gabon Railway into the country's hinterland to Lopé, Lambaréné and the hills of Franceville.

The national park that encompassed Lopé was one of the few places in the world where it was possible to view both forest elephants and gorillas. Bats hung from the overhanging eaves of my hotel's chalets. Little had changed in centuries and to walk with a guide through the stifling heat of the forest canopy to the grassy clearings known as *bais* was to walk in the footsteps of Mary Kingsley, the nineteenth-century English explorer who, in refusing to be weighed down by crinoline and Victorian expectation to travel alone into wild lands inhabited by Fang cannibals, needed a courage far greater than my own. In her day, there was no rail line cutting inland to the Ogooué River at Mount Brazza, a peak that looked much the same now as it did in Kingsley's photographs – a velvety boil on the landscape, the colour of drying straw, now crowned with the lancet of a communications tower.

I had come to see wildlife, but I found myself drawn to stories, such as that of Nobel Peace Prize laureate Albert Schweitzer who journeyed inland from the coast at a time when there were barely any roads leading into the interior. He and his wife travelled alone with their beloved upright piano to treat locals who had no access to medical care, taking chickens or jobs in kind as payment for his services. The Albert Schweitzer Hospital he set up was still going strong in Lambaréné, more than one hundred years later, and was still almost as remote – a long and cramped bush-taxi ride from Libreville across the equator, or a speedboat journey along the Ogooué from Gabon's second city, Port-Gentil, which was itself cut off by water from the rest of the country.

Travelling alone along the river in search of Kingsley, Schweitzer and myself, interacting with locals and undergoing a wealth of experiences which had nothing to do with the wildlife I had come to see, gave me the confidence to undertake much greater solo adventures in later years. In short, travelling solo changed me, and I'll be forever grateful to myself for taking the risk of buying that airline ticket for a journey no-one wanted to accompany me on.

Ian Packham is an adventurer, award-winning travel writer and speaker. His biggest adventure was the first solo and unassisted circumnavigation of Africa by public transport, a journey of thirteen months and 25,000 miles. Since then he  has travelled the length of Sri Lanka's longest river on foot and by kayak, walked the coast of the Isle of Man and travelled through Scandinavia using a 1960s guidebook. His next adventure will be travelling through North Africa and Italy retracing the steps of his great uncle during World War II.

The Unexpected Consolations of Getting it All Wrong

Kirsty Fergusson

There were four of us, confined to the tedium of a provincial French town of impeccable bourgeois character for the duration of the school year. Paris was only an hour away by train, but the meagre salaries accorded to twenty-year-old English lycée assistants made all but the odd day out impossible, spent mostly wandering the streets or nursing tiny cups of coffee while observing the city and its inhabitants. A cosy comradeship developed, ensuring that however much we walked and talked, we never stepped outside the comfort of our collective experiences, never engaged – beyond superficial communication – with the world around us.

Autumn dissolved into winter and we all went home to England for the Christmas holidays and returned, hungover and homesick, to start the frosty January of 1981 in sullen classrooms and the smoke-filled teachers' common room.

Neither Sue nor Philip nor Mike would come to Paris that first weekend we were back. Sue had a cold, while Philip had acquired a mysterious girlfriend and Mike had an invitation to lunch with the family of one of his students. It was freezing, but I longed to escape the shuttered town. A small sum of Christmas money was burning a hole in my pocket, too. Descending from the local train in the steamy Gare de l'Est I lingered, reading the departure boards with awe: Berlin. Munich. Vienna. Budapest. Moscow. On impulse, I went to the ticket office and picked up timetables and a leaflet advertising InterRail cards for students. An American couple wearing huge rucksacks interrupted my reading. Go to Luxembourg to buy your card, they urged. You only get cheap travel outside the country where you're living and you'll save a heap of money if you buy it in Luxembourg. I was confused and pointed out I didn't live in Luxembourg. They looked at me as though I was a rather dim child.

So I spent that Saturday travelling to Luxembourg and back, blushing to remember the lies I had told, amazed that no-one had questioned the manifestly manufactured address and invented place of work. But I had my card, valid for one month, and that was all that mattered.

I knew that I was wasting my time trying to persuade any or all of the others to join me on the three weekends I planned to spend visiting Vienna, Munich and Berlin. The last journey of the month would be back to England at half price for the February half term. Friday and Sunday nights were to be spent on the train, thus reducing the need for accommodation to only one night while I was away. As soon as lessons were finished on a Friday afternoon I would race to the station for the early evening train to Paris and cross platforms to an adventure. If my timetables were accurate and trains ran on time, I might just squeak back to school ahead of my first class – which mercifully started late on Monday mornings. Fifty francs for food, plus bread sneaked from Friday's lunch; 120 francs for accommodation. About fifteen quid. That was my budget and I had no choice but to stick to it.

Vienna turned out to be an inauspicious start. Greyish mounds of snow lay heaped along the streets. The icy pavements had been spread with cinders, over which an elderly population, muffled against the cold in grey and black, shuffled carefully. The vast monuments of the Habsburg Empire looked sorry and grimed by age, too. I found refuge and some degree of warmth in the Kunsthistorisches Museum, devouring every detail of the busy Brueghels and discovering Klimt in the frescoed halls. The youth hostel was almost empty, the Danube wasn't blue and my suede desert boots leaked. I talked to no-one and realised that I had only begun to taste the true flavour of homesickness in France.

In Munich the following weekend, the snow had turned to slush. Caught out by an overpriced breakfast, by Saturday evening I was starving and too nervous to enter alone the kind of hostelries that oozed cheerful Germanic sounds suggesting the happy consumption of beer and sausages. Eventually I found a quiet café and studied the menu in the window, formulating a brilliant plan – I would order the longest word on the menu with the cheapest price tag beside it. This turned out to be *Leberknödelsuppe*, which I imaginatively construed as 'lovelysomethingsoup'. The greasy, watery broth containing a pungent clot of minced liver and flaccid noodles must have received some extra salt from the tears I quietly shed as I spooned the beastly stuff into my mouth. Perhaps the waitress thought these were tears born of fond nostalgia for the food of my childhood because she returned with an anxious smile and another bowlful, kindly heedless of my teary protests.

Berlin was my last chance to get the hang of solo travel before my InterRail card expired. I'd already learned the art of rendering mishap – if not quite misery – into amusing anecdotes for those I'd left behind, but I was far from convinced that I was born to be a solitary adventurer. It was shortly after nine in the morning when I found myself at the desk of the tourist office in West Berlin's main station. A cheap room? Just for one night? Impossible! Didn't I realise that West Berlin was hosting a major trade expo and every room in the city had been booked for weeks in advance? And the youth hostel was closed. It was snowing heavily outside. I shuffled my feet and said Oh. Oh dear. The tourist officer sighed, scribbled an address and passed it across the counter. She might have something. Worth a try. Here's a map.

I stood at last before a tall, narrow townhouse. A very old, very small woman opened the door and looked at me beadily. Was there a room available? She didn't answer, but beckoned impatiently. Come. Tea's getting cold. Upstairs I found myself in a drawing room crowded with heavy furniture; a grand piano stood in the floor-length window. Another equally tiny and aged woman sat in an armchair before a silver tray, teapot, cups and saucers. The two old ladies quizzed me in heavily-accented English. American? No. English? Yes. Tea? Thank you. Cream? Well, milk, please, if you've got it. So you *are* English. Only the English have milk and pour it first. So you can have a room. I don't like Americans. Now you will play the piano.

I hardly stirred from the house that day. I was allocated a camp bed, hidden behind a curtain under the stairs, beside a bathroom of mausoleum-like proportions, acoustics and grandeur. My piano repertoire consisted of the first – and easy – bit of 'Für Elise' and 'Camptown Races'. I played both pieces to my surprisingly enthusiastic audience of two. Again and again, the old birds insisted I play the same two pieces until I pleaded exhaustion. And hungry, yes? I nodded, though my look of anguish mixed with gratitude came from the appalling thought that they might be about to offer me a steaming bowl of Leberknödelsuppe. The first old lady stood at the long window and pointed down at the street. Hungry. When our city was besieged, a horse fell between the shafts of its cart right there. In five minutes it was no more than a skeleton. We stripped its flesh while it still breathed. Hunger is a terrible thing. Don't go to the East. You have no reason to. Stay here.

The following day, ignoring her advice, I walked to Checkpoint Charlie. The wall, the graffiti, the guards. Nothing to do except look. I returned to the house to collect my bag, still wondering about the woman's aversion to Americans, but when I arrived, she wasn't in the mood for talking. What have you seen? You went there? Why? That was a stupid thing to do. She said goodbye crossly and didn't give me the change I was expecting from my fifty marks.

The train had come from Moscow and was overcrowded. I pushed my way down the length of it, asked the conductor, but there were no seats remaining. I stood in the corridor beside my rucksack, leaning on the window, watching the snowy night flash past. At least it was warm. An hour passed and I dozed on my feet. Then, the glass door of the compartment behind me slid open. Six earnest faces entreated me to come in; my bag was hoisted on to the rack and space made for me. They were Russian – six men aged from eighteen to eighty as far as I could tell, dressed in double-breasted brown or black suits with turn-up trousers, emitting a strong smell of camphor. Homburgs and cardboard suitcases were stacked overhead. One spoke a little English. I spoke a little Russian, thanks to an eccentric teacher at school who had offered the language of Tolstoy as an alternative to German or Spanish. The beaming men all worked on a collective farm somewhere near Moscow and were being rewarded for high yields and exemplary Soviet spirit with a week in Cologne, all paid for.

They were very proud and touchingly excited. But despite heroic efforts on both sides of the linguistic divide, we soon exhausted the possibilities of conversation. It was during the last and seemingly fatal conversational lull that I noticed the temperature had dropped dramatically and I was starting to shiver. The heating in our carriage had broken down.

'*Nichevo!*' A smile and a wagging finger. 'It doesn't matter!' Glances were exchanged and cautiously a brown paper bag was extracted from a case. Inside, a bottle of vodka. They passed it round, carefully wiping it before my turn came. There was no backing out. Next, a packet of Leningrad cigarettes was produced – filterless, maize-paper brown and curiously oval in cross section. They all lit up, and then with great courtesy the packet was offered to me. Again, I submitted to their hopeful anticipation. Will she refuse? I didn't smoke. Yet I took one and six hands flew out with a light. '*Ona kurit!*' 'She smokes!' They sighed with relief and passed a second bottle of vodka around.

When I awoke, I found I was lying face down across all the seats on one side of the compartment. It was still cold, but someone had thoughtfully covered me with my coat. The floor met my gaze. It was speckled with crushed brown cigarette butts and an empty bottle rolled back and forth as the train thundered on. It was just getting light. I frowned and lifted my head. It thumped a little. On the three seats facing me sat a man, a woman and a plump boy of about eight. They were all chewing slowly and silently and a strong smell of smoked sausage confused with stale smoke and damp wool thickened the atmosphere. The family ate steadily and regarded me without expression. I sat up and asked where we were. Belgium. Then we all looked down at the rolling bottle. I picked it up and stuffed it into my rucksack. After that no-one spoke until we arrived in Paris.

I saw my three friends at lunchtime in the school canteen. Philip's mystery girlfriend turned out to be Sue, of course. Mike grinned. You look rough! What went wrong this time? I told them about the old ladies' tea party and my improvised piano recital, about the poor horse in the siege and the soldiers in fur hats at Checkpoint Charlie; I showed them the bottle of vodka with the Cyrillic script on the label and laughed about the happy Russian farmers. I should have come with you after all, said Mike, and I turned my head away so he couldn't see how important it was that he hadn't.

Kirsty Fergusson's love of solo travel remains undiminished. This was written on an overnight train from Paris to Bologna in the luxury of an empty sleeper compartment. She is the author of the award-winning Bradt title, *Cornwall*, in the Slow Travel series. She is, however, quite sociable and spends much of the year running lovely tours all over Europe for readers of *The Oldie* magazine.

Of Red Earth and Fruit Bats

Amanda Lumley

I was finally on the Tube en route to London Heathrow to catch my flight to Australia. I was late, so much so that my name was broadcast over the intercom at the airport. A panicked goodbye to my mother, who wept under a fake tree while my sister comforted her, and I was running for the plane. Ironic that one of the most important experiences of my life almost never happened because I was so reluctant to leave that I delayed getting on the Tube.

Despite all my preparations I was suddenly terrified to be travelling for a year, by myself, in another country. This was twenty years ago, before cell phones, instant messaging and everyday access to computers. But, as with so many things in life where our intuitive selves determine what's best for us, I knew I had to go to expand my comfort zone.

I started off easy, in Sydney, where I found temping work. I shared a hostel room with other solo travellers, spent hours exploring the city on foot and read *Lord of the Rings* lying on the grass in a park in the October spring sun, the complex, warbling song of the Australian magpie a constant backdrop. When friends travelling from England decided to make Australia part of their itinerary we spent three months sharing a Victorian house in the trendy Paddington, or 'Paddo', area – a house which turned out to be, revoltingly, infested first by fleas and then cockroaches. Sydney is a mass of jumbled memories:

of frangipani trees lining the streets, their delicately fragrant white and yellow flowers covering the pavement as they fell; of cheap meals out, often strolling the streets afterwards in the evening. We'd find ourselves walking under trees occupied by bats, chattering and bickering above as discarded bits of fruit, flowers and their guano fell on our heads. Australians really did say 'g'day!' and 'no worries!' and mail deliverers really did wear shorts to work on their rounds. The sun shone almost every day. Everyone seemed to be in a perennially good mood.

I'd found myself in a comfortable routine existence once again, though, albeit an exotic one, and knew then it was time to move on, alone. I'd joined the Wilderness Society in Sydney as a volunteer and they passed along a coveted opportunity to assist in a flying fox, or fruit bat, research project at Cape Tribulation, deep in the heart of the ancient Daintree rainforest in far north Queensland. It was irresistible – free accommodation in a remote region I'd never even heard of in return for counting fig trees, whose fruit the bats favoured. Within a short time I said goodbye to Sydney, friends and a burgeoning relationship and spent three days on buses travelling to Cairns.

Hours evaporated watching endless tracts of red earth, scrubby bushes and an overwhelmingly vast blue sky from my seat window. As the sun began to set, the rust-coloured terrain turned by degrees to exquisite purple hues. I saw Aboriginal people walking by the side of dusty roads in towns we passed through; two men behind my seat laughed and horrifyingly mimicked the act of shooting a gun at them.

From Cairns I was picked up by the husband-and-wife team who ran the research project and we bumped our way in their Land Rover up what was then a rough dirt road to Cape Tribulation. At the research centre I was introduced to a resident fruit bat, Sammy, rescued but unable to live again in the wild. As I walked through the front door he flew from the far side of the room and landed on my feet. I looked down, he looked up and then, using the little claws at the tip of each digit, he started to pull his way up my jeans and over my top until we were almost nose to nose. I stood absolutely still. I had no idea what else to do. His dark, golden-ruffed, foxy, amber-eyed face studied mine. 'He likes you,' the wife said. It seemed I'd passed some unspoken test of approval by bat and humans alike.

My home for the next two weeks was a trailer in a clearing of the forest. Each night I tucked the mosquito netting under my mattress, more for the snakes and spiders than anything else. Above my bed a large web hung where a beautifully marked yellow and black arachnid lived; from behind the chest of drawers (which I never dared to use; I had no wish to open a drawer to find god knows what inside) a huntsman spider emerged every night. Walking through the forest I'd often spot a Children's python, its distinctive mottling giving it away. On a guided tour of the forest one evening we observed perhaps a dozen pairs of eyes glinting red in the torchlight – crocodiles lurking in the nearby creeks. On breaks from counting fig trees, I'd walk through the forest to emerge at the very edge of the beach. Locals talked of a great white shark stalking the waters off the headland. The thought of sharks and estuarine crocodiles, 'salties' as they were known, was enough to deter any idea of swimming.

It was alarming. But it was also remarkable to live in the rainforest, a capsule of flora and fauna quite different from the rest of the country. And I became very comfortable with bats. Apart from Sammy, other rescued fruit bats, often orphans, had found a home here. Protected by netting from predatory snakes, intelligent and curious, they'd swarm over to me, delicately pulling my hair with their claws as I entered their enclosure each morning to hand-feed them chopped-up bananas, mangoes and papaya.

This newfound confidence with wildlife came in handy shortly after I'd left Cape Tribulation. As I ate dinner one night in an almost deserted hostel in Cairns, a tiny bat suddenly flew in an open window and crashed at my feet. Without thinking I bent down, gently pinned its wings with one hand to prevent it flying into a wall, took it outside, held it upside down and waited until its feet found the tree branch I raised it up to. Slowly I took away my hand and within a second or two it had flown off. It was a magical moment. There was no other word for it.

I spent months after Cape Tribulation on farms near the Queensland coast, picking green beans off conveyor belts and rescuing the occasional green tree frog that had somehow ended up there as well. Groups of us from the hostel would get up before dawn broke to hitch to outlying farms and start planting peppers in the red soil, backs breaking from bending over for hours, before it got too hot. I took a side trip to New Zealand, hiking and working for several months before being pulled back to the intensity of Australia. I knew I needed to see and experience more, but my time had vaporised.

And so I found myself in a very hot telephone box on a baking street in Townsville in northeastern Australia. Sweat beaded on my body as the sun beat in through the glass while I waited breathlessly for the voice on the other end of the line to decide my fate for the next six months. I'd asked for an extension on my one-year work visa which was about to expire. Desperately I recounted to the customs officer how much I loved being in Australia, how the extraordinary environment had affected and inspired me; I said that I wanted to write about my time here, to share with others the impact the country had had on me. I wanted to experience just a little more. I was lucky. Either my argument was persuasive or the customs official was particularly kind. I got another six months.

I used that extra time well. In Kakadu National Park black flies swarmed, attempting to breach ears, nose, mouth and eyes. The Dreamtime was much in evidence here, the creation stories of the Aboriginal people unfolding in age-old rock art. And in Shark Bay I stood at the edge of a tract of rare marine stromatolites, living fossils that have helped to unravel the history of life on earth.

A year and a half after I'd started my journey, I was sad to leave but ready to go home, grateful for the experiences that had been offered to me. Australia is extreme in so many ways – the heat, the number of things that can bite or sting you, often fatally, its vast size, the intense light and colours and the sense of the ancient it projects. It had made me a braver, more confident person. I'd become, in my own modest way, a bit of an adventurer.

Three years after graduating from university **Amanda Lumley** left England for Australia. Inspired by her experiences she spent only a short time back in the UK before taking off again. A trip to India was later followed by a permanent  move to British Columbia, Canada, where she now lives with her husband, mountain biking, cross-country skiing, hiking and camping whenever she has the chance.

Tips

Travel light – feel free to move about without the hassle of lots of luggage. *Elspeth Cardy*

Change your plans on a whim; be influenced by people and experiences along the way. Chances taken are the essence of travel and exploration… My only travel regrets are chances not taken. I was once offered a free plane ride to the Galapagos if I didn't mind spending it with cow carcasses and no windows. I was worried I might be airsick and how would I get back again, so I declined. Now, still never having been to the Galapagos, I can't believe a possible vomit or two held me back. *Claire Morsman*

Walk, walk, walk until you're so tired you sleep off your anxiety. *Matt Dawson*

People are generally kind and like to be helpful, so don't be afraid to ask. When a plump Indian Mama put her finger on the knot for me as I was struggling to tie string round a package at Calcutta airport, we both ended up beaming happily. *Janice Booth*

Brief Encounters

✥ ✥ ✥

A brief encounter with other travellers or locals can transform the solo travel experience, and these stories show how easily and simply that can happen – if you allow it to. From the perspective of youth or age, the result is the same; it could happen on a beach in Fiji, around a dining table or at an ancient site. Nicole Teufel, still a teenager when she travels to Vladivostok alone, is naturally wary of a cab driver who seems to fit the bill of a crook, but 'I suddenly felt embarrassed and a little ashamed. He was the kindest cab driver I'd ever known.' Janice Booth reflects on a brief meeting that taught her a lesson: 'travel involved not only landscapes and tourist attractions…but also interaction with local people. During my fifty-plus travelling years since then, those human encounters have always been my greatest pleasure.'

Eight Hours in Fiji

Matt Dawson

Once, when a month shy of my nineteenth birthday, I found myself stuck in Fiji. Stuck seems an odd choice of word for a destination many would pay thousands to visit, but it was an eight-hour wait for my connecting flight to Vancouver, where I was eager to meet up with a friend I hadn't seen in two years. Fiji felt like an inconvenience, especially considering a day sunbathing wasn't really my thing.

Legally a man, mentally a boy, and crippled by an endless feeling of embarrassment that made approaching anyone an ordeal – even asking a waiter for the menu was an emotionally draining experience – I had spent the previous three months cycle touring Australia with a friend, Will. He was more outgoing, happy to meet people and incorporate others into a group. He had a calm knack of social engagement that was easy to idolise, not just because of the ease with which his words flowed, but also the way small talk wouldn't tire him to the point of coma. Will was exactly the kind of person us introverts love to hide behind. Combine this with cycling being the ultimate way to shun social engagement for hours, if not days, on end and my plan to become more outgoing through the medium of travel had been less than a success.

Now, though, I was alone in a foreign country for the very first time. As I stood in the arrivals hall of Nadi International Airport, I toyed with the idea of passing the long wait in a coffee shop with my eyes fixed firmly on the pages of a book. I knew this was unacceptable behaviour for a man whose family now considered him an explorer, so I took a deep breath, grabbed my rucksack and made for the exit.

The slow walk to the taxi rank elicited the kind of internal panic most reserve for a life-changing interview. Of course, it was ridiculous to be so nervous about something so normal as ordering a taxi. I'd read that it was amygdala in the brain's temporal lobe, a key component in our fear and anxiety circuitry, that was partly to blame. Right now this tight bundle of neurons had decided that the best possible response to the situation was moist hands and a dry mouth. I couldn't help but wonder what it knew that the rest of me didn't.

'Where you going?' the taxi driver asked.

My knowledge of Fiji stopped at idyllic beaches and the one thing I knew for sure was that I didn't fancy lazing on a sunbed for hours. I swigged some water. What was there to see in Fiji? I panicked.

'The beach,' I said.

'Which one?'

I couldn't deny this was a good question. The taxi driver was a short, big man. Some might call him solid, others obese. He had a large, inviting, toothy smile that helped to put me at ease, which was exactly the opposite feeling elicited by his taxi – it was sun-kissed and battered. In between the rust there were hints of green with white and orange racing stripes. The wing mirrors stuck out from the bonnet and I couldn't decide if this was the actual design or whether they had been moved for aesthetic purposes.

'A nice one,' I said with a faint smile.

It was just after nine in the morning and the taxi began to heat up as we made our way through town. As I puffed my cheeks and congratulated myself on mission accomplished, I noticed that the window winder sat on the seat beside me. With the black leatherette seat covers ripped and shredded as though attacked by a velociraptor, the speedometer stuck on thirty and frayed wires dangling in front of my eyes, the inside of the taxi was as run down as its outer shell. The only thing remotely new was the sound system that filled every inch of the boot and blared out Motown classics. We drove through rolling green countryside, passing fields of livestock and small villages, bopping our heads to the Jackson Five. I say drove, but that does the word an injustice. We'd stalled four times before even leaving the confines of the airport.

At this point, those with a little more social aptitude would have spoken up. Maybe even clambered out of the taxi and cut their losses. They definitely would have if they'd spotted the gear stick, which was rocking back and forth to such a violent extent that twice it flicked the stereo and changed the radio station. For me, such an epiphany only came twenty minutes later, when we hit a cow.

The driver's attention had been diverted somewhat by the dodgy gear stick breaking off in his hand. He stared at it with the disbelief of a man who has just eaten an entire packet of biscuits when only intending to have one. This moment of confusion was ample time for the cow to back its rear end out into the road and for the wing mirror to give it a mighty slap.

We pulled over near a banana plantation and I sprinted back to check on the cow, which was staring at the dislodged wing mirror with heroic indifference.

'I give you ten per cent off,' the driver shouted above the screeches of The Supremes and a series of metal twangs caused by his desperate attempt to hammer the gear stick back in with the wing mirror.

'Ten per cent!' I yelled. 'I'm not getting back in that car with you.'

'Twenty per cent.'

'Show me your driver's licence.'

'Please, I take you to the next town.'

'How far's that?'

The driver shrugged. 'About three miles.'

'I'll walk.'

I grabbed my rucksack and headed off down the road flanked by an ocean of banana plantations, the enormous leaves towering over me. The sun hung high in the sky, mocking my weakness with the intensity of its heat. I had no water, no food and no idea where I was. I also still had my jeans on, so decided to change into shorts. At the very moment my trousers dropped down, another taxi swung around the corner and pulled up in front of me. A young Australian girl with short blonde hair popped her head out the sunroof. My face flushed as red as my underwear.

'Sexy undies, mate,' she said. 'Which way you headed?'

'The beach.'

'Us too. Hop in.'

The second taxi was cleaner and driven by a younger man wearing a black baseball cap. In the back was the girl, Steph, and her burly boyfriend, Brandon. As luck would have it, we were on the same flight to Vancouver.

'Some taxis are not good,' the driver said when I recounted my woes. 'Look for the licence,' he added, tapping his knuckle on the window to indicate his.

'Vishal here knows a great beach,' Brandon said, giving the driver a mighty slap on the back.

'A beach like no other,' Vishal said.

'Cocktails by the shore,' Steph added.

'The best cocktails in all of Fiji,' Vishal promised.

My idea of an idyllic beach is probably not far off yours – golden sand, deep blue sky, palm trees, a gently lapping ocean and the kind of silence that could cure high blood pressure. Vishal had very different ideas. If the building site that was pumping its waste into the sea wasn't bad enough, the colour of the sand probably was.

'It's black,' Steph said, flicking the grains with her flip-flop.

Vishal sensed the Australian's displeasure. He adjusted his cap and shrugged. 'But all beaches are golden.'

'Exactly.'

'Now you can tell people you've been to a volcanic beach.'

'Not sure how impressive that is, mate.'

'Please, I show you. Follow me. Cocktails on a volcanic beach. What a story!' Vishal clapped his hands.

My amygdala was less than impressed, but follow Vishal we did. With two hours down, there wasn't really much time to do anything else. It was a further fifteen-minute walk along the shore before we reached the cocktail bar. I'm being generous, because it was more a wooden hut, with a few deckchairs arranged around an old tractor tyre-come-table. A Fijian man, no older than twenty and sporting the faintest of moustaches, was slumped in one of the chairs fanning himself with a newspaper.

'This is Paul,' Vishal said, 'the best cocktail waiter in Fiji.' Such bold words knocked the waiter from his slumber.

'Paul wouldn't happen to be your brother, would he?' Brandon asked.

'No, no, no,' Vishal said with a laugh that fully acknowledged the cynicism in Brandon's voice. 'My cousin.'

Now here's the thing. What happened next makes it very difficult for me to deny that Paul may well be the best cocktail waiter in Fiji. For a start he shimmied up a tree with the agility of a lemur to hack down a bunch of coconuts. He had all the moves, repeatedly flicking the spirit bottles behind his back, throwing limes across the bar straight into the glasses and chopping coconuts with a twenty-yard knife throw. He even tried to teach us and seemed to care very little when a rum bottle smashed to the floor. For four hours we drank cocktails that tasted so spectacular we hardly noticed the bubbly white sewage drifting on to the darkened shore.

At this point, those of you with a rudimentary grasp of maths will have spotted a problem – we had lost track of time and our flight was leaving in two hours.

'Where's Vishal? Where's Vishal?' Steph repeated as we sprinted back towards the cab.

Back at the building site, the taxi driver was nowhere to be seen. Attention turned to his cousin.

'No problem, I'll find you a taxi,' Paul promised. And he did. One that blared out Motown classics and sported just one wing mirror.

In fairness, all went well for the first half an hour. Then the gear stick popped out again, leaving us stuck in second gear. Our race to the airport turned into a grindingly noisy crawl, placated with push starts at every junction.

Steph looked at her watch. 'This is like a horrible nightmare,' she said. 'We're not going to make it.'

A day later, I was in a bar in Vancouver enjoying a few beers with my friend, Mike. I told him about the taxis, the cow, the black sand, the cocktails, the slow-motion race to the airport and how the plane had been delayed three hours anyway.

'Bet you wish you'd stayed at the airport, read your book,' Mike observed.

We both laughed, but deep inside I couldn't have felt more different. For the first time in a long while the social anxiety that so often draped over me had lifted. My lack of engagement with the world wasn't doing me any favours, but going it alone for those few hours in Fiji had made me new friends and begun to release me from the grasp of the only person ever holding me back – myself.

Matt Dawson is a writer living in London. Since Fiji, he has wandered with wonder through countries in Europe, Asia, Africa and the Americas, often alone. In 2015, he was a finalist in the Bradt and *Independent on Sunday* travel-writing competition.

Abroad

Janice Booth

November, 1961. I was twenty-two, a professional stage manager, emerging from two gruelling years of touring with six different productions to theatres the length and breadth of the country. I badly needed a break, and somewhere well away from Britain.

The trouble was, I didn't really know how holidays worked. I was an only child, and except at boarding school I'd never spent leisure time with anyone but my parents. Stage management hadn't allowed time for socialising, and I had no experience of saying to a friend – of whom I hadn't many long-term ones anyway – 'Shall we go away somewhere?' and making joint plans. It didn't seem much fun alone. My mother, despite feeling miserably sick on the cross-Channel ferries, had gamely taken me to France and Germany in my teens to practise my school languages, so at least I knew about the hotels, unfamiliar trains, border formalities and frustrating queues that 'going abroad' involved. But it was still frightening, and I needed help to get started.

A travel company in London's Regent Street provided it. The airline map on its wall showed a convenient combination of direct British European Airways flights to Gibraltar and Tangier that appealed to me, so I asked the agent to book me a week's stay in each place with flights and hotels. Several phone calls and handwritten air tickets later, everything was fixed. I'd never flown before, but the BOAC *Travellers Digest* enthusiastically claimed: 'Even within a week or two you can cross oceans, pack your holiday with a globe-trotter's impressions, and return with a hundred exotic memories.'

Well, maybe. I got my travellers' cheques and presented myself, rather gloomily, at the BEA West London Air Terminal in Cromwell Road at 4 a.m. on a wet, cold, December morning. A coach then drove me and a handful of other silent, sleepy passengers through rainy darkness to the airport. I have no memory of the actual flight, but evidently I arrived safely – in Gibraltar, that rocky little chunk of Britain clinging to the edge of Spain. Despite its deliberate air of Englishness, it was further abroad than I'd ever been before and I was finally travelling alone.

My hotel was the old and stately Bristol, where my parents had stayed briefly in 1928. My single bedroom with its high, ornate ceiling was cold and the bed was hard, but its view across a medley of rooftops and scattered palm trees to the harbour was satisfactorily unlike home. The ordeal of meals alone in the silent and formal restaurant (I remember a lot of thick brown gravy) was brightened when one of the younger stiff-shirted waiters summoned up a surreptitious smile.

On my first morning, mist hung over the peak, and I felt very unsure how this supposedly exciting adventure should begin. Sitting alone in the hotel garden in watery sunshine, I listened to the birdsong and chatter and the occasional revving vehicle; then I ventured out into the main street, where small shops designed to appeal to tourists jostled shoulder to shoulder. The town guide (I still have it, along with my detailed fifty-five-year-old diary) praised the 'variety and stock of merchandise' and the 'charm of colour and elegance of some antique shops', so I browsed for a while, until the colours began to seem garish and some of the merchandise tawdry.

A favourite childhood treat had been visiting Alfred, the gorilla at Bristol Zoo, so next on my list was to climb the Rock and meet the famous Barbary apes. But they were scruffy and aggressive, and I flinched from the leathery and semi-human little hands that grabbed slyly at whatever took their fancy – in my case the belt of my jacket, which got thoroughly chewed. I could imagine my mother warning me about fleas. I skipped the historic caves and tunnels; they were dank and I wasn't interested enough in their origins. The time seemed likely to drag and I wondered whether 'going on holiday' was really such a big deal. Maybe a sea trip would help?

So I caught the ferry across to Tangier and back, just for the ride, glad of my experience on the cross-Channel ferries at home. Away from the Rock's shadow the sea sparkled blue and the sun was hot on my skin. I leaned contentedly on the rail, buffeted by the wind and scanning the ocean – stout Cortez in search of new lands. Three dolphins broke up through the water, twisted among curls of foam and sank smoothly down into the green shadows. Tangier's docks looked uninviting so I stayed on board, watching the to and fro of passengers and cars, before heading back.

How incongruously middle-aged my twenty-two-year-old self must have seemed, reading her book in the manicured gardens and sedately visiting the recommended sights. Probably I wore a skirt, and stockings, and sensible shoes. I was travelling in the same manner as my parents, whose example was the only one I had, when I should have been giggling with friends and amassing the 'hundred exotic memories' the BOAC handbook had promised.

Then I met Pio, and 'abroad' took on a different face.

Because I'd enjoyed the sea trip to Tangier, I decided to take the Algeciras ferry and explore a bit of Spain; the country was linked in my mind to a little red leather-covered notebook, with *Mi Diario* stamped in gold on the front, that my father had brought me from Madrid when I was nine. I was leaning on the rail watching the Rock recede, when a voice behind me made some banal comment about the mist hanging over the peak. I turned. 'A short, shrivelled, shapeless little man,' my careful diary cruelly reminds me, 'with thin hair and a tight pointed face. Small dull hazel eyes. Cheap, worn, brownish suit and scuffed leather shoes. A huge wristwatch on one spindly arm.' Probably only a few years older than myself, he stood there uncertainly, focusing on me through a kind of magnifying jeweller's eyeglass that fitted into one eye.

Not quite Gregory Peck, then, but politeness prevailed. I abandoned the sea and the Spanish coastline and engaged in conversation. He was going to Algeciras 'for a walk', he said, 'because Gibraltar is small and I like to get away.' Only the wider world interested him; his home was unimportant. He knew about many distant countries, but only from books. Living with his parents and three brothers in three rooms and a kitchen, he explained, 'I do not have a room of my own. I have no privacy. If I had a room of my own, I would be like a king with a castle!'

Predictably, he worked as a clerk. 'At one time I wanted to go into business,' he explained. 'I took a course in business management from the London Correspondence School. I passed it and got a diploma, but it was no use. Nobody wanted my diploma, so I am still a clerk.' There was no self-pity. This small, nondescript person simply accepted the hand he had been dealt.

I guided him through the border formalities that every trip outside Gibraltar required, as he was too short-sighted to read the signs. Then I said goodbye – but somehow he stayed and we wandered slowly through the quiet town. He knew it well, pointing out buildings or views he thought might please me. 'White houses,' says my diary, 'crimson flowers, the pattern of shutters in the streets. Windows reflected in the ripples of a harbour inlet. Sun white with heat throwing golden shadows; life is on holiday among the orange trees. Black-shawled women and children with restless eyes.'

We paused in some gardens, gracious and shady. 'I am fond of gardens,' he said. 'You might say it is a weakness. I don't know the names of the trees, but I like to watch their shape. They are graceful, how the trunks stretch upwards to the leaves.' His accent, his careful English and his awareness of small pleasures were oddly touching.

At lunchtime I refused his invitation to a restaurant, and sat on a low stone wall beside an orange grove to eat a sandwich and enjoy the peace. The town was dozing in siesta. Only buzzing insects broke the silence and the sun soaked into my bones. After a while Pio returned, scanning with his eyeglass to locate me. He told me about Spanish food and what dishes I should eat 'next time', and on the way back to the ferry he took me to a secluded little strip of sandy beach. 'This is a good place for you to remember,' he said. 'I like to come here because of the quietness, but always alone. No-one else is interested.'

On the return I helped him through the border formalities again, this small, shabby, incongruous square peg whose mind so far outstripped his body. He asked me to meet him the following day, but I lied that I'd already made arrangements. So he gave me his phone number, 'in case you might want to get in touch with me again,' and I wrote it down; but I knew, and he knew, that I would never use it. He was so lonely, and I still feel guilty. I had no hard-won correspondence school diploma in business management, so why should my life be so much better than his? And with my comfortable, cocooning single bedroom I'd been 'a king with a castle' all my life.

Two days later I was in Tangier and, for all its sadness, that day with Pio had left me unexpectedly strengthened. It had given me a role. I knew he'd enjoyed my company, and I'd learnt that travel involved not only landscapes and tourist attractions (as it had in my teens with my mother), but also interaction with local people. During my fifty-plus travelling years since then, those human encounters have always been my greatest pleasure.

My small hotel was clean and friendly, and I spoke to other guests. I hired a car, a red VW Beetle, and explored the surprisingly leafy countryside outside the town, eating a picnic lunch beside a stream and chatting to some shy-eyed, barefoot children who broke into giggles as they scampered away over the grass. I wandered down narrow streets, past houses with high carved doorways and hidden courtyards with fountains and tumbling vines. In the dizzying, crowded central souk, hands of all shades and sizes beckoned me to buy; I soaked up the noise and the smells and the colours, tasted strange sweets and admired delicate jewellery. A lad offered himself as a 'guide' and took me to what he said was his uncle's shop, where I bought a leather pouffe that later stained my carpets red. Now I was travelling as myself rather than as an offshoot of my parents, and the sense of freedom was tremendous. 'Abroad' had become my own back yard, and the whole world – and its people – lay ahead of me, waiting to be explored.

Janice Booth has since spent time in, and written about, Timbuktu and Rwanda, among many other solo travels. She is co-author of the *Bradt Guide to Rwanda*, which has helped the country's tourist industry so much in its recovery from the 1994 genocide. Now she lives peacefully in Devon, running a  poetry reading group, appreciating her bus pass and trying to resist pasties and clotted cream. With Hilary Bradt, she has co-written two of Bradt's Slow Travel guides: *East Devon & the Jurassic Coast*, and *South Devon & Dartmoor*.

The Ghan

Debbie Parrott

Oh no, not him. Or her. Please. Not the child.

Down the aisle tottered a small boy. I held my breath, but he carried on.

I had just flown across the world, successfully fending off all armrest challenges, so why was I buckling now on an internal flight to Adelaide? It was simple. Panic. Prior to this Australia trip I always knew who would be sitting next to me.

A lady slid in gracefully beside me. Elegant and manicured hands smoothed her skirt before retrieving a laptop and placing it on her knees. She percolated confidence. My frown tightened and, avoiding all eye contact, I opened my book to read and reread the same page.

I did not want to be doing this: *The Ghan*, Ayers Rock and Perth for Christmas.

Yet the scorching view over that vast desert as we flew into Sydney had made me gasp. The clouds had glowing edges and through the gaps the sun's rays had rushed to sear the land a garish, burning red, as if the outside of a rainbow had fallen off and floated down to earth.

Adelaide Airport may be small and easy to navigate, but the case was just as heavy to wheel so it was a relief when I found a taxi.

'G'day. I'll take that,' said the driver and, with no more effort than it would take him to lift a beer, put my bag into the boot of his car.

'Where to, ma'am?'

'The station, please.'

'You goin' on *The Afghan Express* all the way to the Top End?'

'I'm catching *The Ghan* to Alice Springs.' *And don't feel you have to talk to me.*

'Good on ya. My great, great grandpa, known as "Two-Gs Grandpa", helped to build that railway. It's why I'm here driving this taxi.'

His brown eyes smiled into the mirror and I let my reply slide into a hole before curiosity hauled it back.

'How come?'

'We-e-ll, in nineteen hundred, just before Queen Vicky choked, Two-Gs Grandpa, aka Akbar Muhammad, came over from Afghanistan. He came with fifty camels cos the Poms couldn't keep horses and buffaloes alive in the desert. Water problem. Camels don't have the same dying issues with the stuff. Poms were desperate to explore the outback and Two-Gs Grandpa was sharp as a shearer. He didn't have any kangaroos loose in his top paddock. He charged big bickies for his camels, made a quid or two and decided to stay. Changed his name to Alec Hammer. I'm Alec Hammersmith – after great grandmother's family from London.'

'Goodness me! What a story.'

'Dead set. I'd tell you more but we're here.'

I was disappointed. It had been only ten minutes, but he was so much more interesting than my guidebook. I caught myself grinning as I walked away. One of the many reasons I had chosen Australia for this particular trip was that I would not have to struggle with the language.

I went to check in, still wondering how the ancestor of a cameleer could so efficiently have slipped me a 'positivity pill'. It didn't last long.

'What do you mean I can't take my case with me?'

'Big pieces must go in the luggage carriage.'

I scowled. The woman smiled indulgently. 'It would have been in the literature that Southern Rail sent you,' she added.

'It most certainly was no...' The flush appeared from nowhere. I remembered reading it.

I should not be doing all this on my own.

I scurried away from the queue, fumbled with locks and opened the case to sort out some overnight necessities. My knickers were on the top. Could everyone see them? Where was the spare bag? At the bottom! I wondered how visible embarrassment was.

Clutching my boarding ticket I strode to the platform where a wall of heat and sun-reflected glare greeted me. I blinked behind my sunglasses. Shining silver carriages snaked away in both directions. I couldn't see the engines at either the head or the tail end. This was a train of anaconda proportions. Before me, a huge red dromedary was embossed on to a shining carriage between the words *THE* and *GHAN*. My heart did a little bounce before bracing.

Where was my carriage? Which direction? Left or right? Thirty-eight degrees was too hot for wasted steps.

'Can I help?'

I thrust my ticket at the uniformed man.

'Down that way, ma'am. Six down. You'll see the number.'

'Thanks,' I said, and as beads of sweat poised to trickle, I headed off.

Having scrambled aboard, I manoeuvred myself and the overnight bag down the corridor. Finding my cabin, I stood in the doorway and took in the snug scale of things – one window, one shelf, one very comfy-looking chair which, I hoped, would later transform into a very comfy bed. It was a single. A *single*. I sat down. Should I slide the door open or shut? I shut it. There was something very reassuring about being wrapped into a small space, a travelling bolthole.

At just after midday a rumbling under the floor signalled that we were on our way. The engines heaved, the carriages juddered and by clunking degrees we rolled out of the station.

Away from Adelaide, the train seemed to comb a parting through the vast, spreading wheat fields. In the distance, the Clare Valley vineyards formed a fringe of soft green and I imagined dangling grapes and a chilled glass of Riesling.

Further on, the towering smokestack at Port Pirie created a contrast with smoke belching from the smelters of silver, lead and zinc. Port Augusta, that trading post for all things outback, flagged us due north, then all beyond was desert. Within minutes the sun was drinking dry, rusty-red earth. Sunset, when it came, stained the sky scarlet and burnished even the scrawniest spinifex bush a vibrant orange so that the desert appeared to be littered with small, burning campfires.

There was an hour before dinner. Could I go to the bar on my own? I had travelled so far already. Surely I could manage a minor sortie like this. Should I take my valuables with me? There was no safe. Should I hide them? Where, though? Yes, no, yes, no, yes... Finally I set off in search of a gin and tonic. I got as far as the door and peered through the glass. The bar was at the far end which meant walking down the whole length of the carriage, right down the middle between all those apparently jolly people. Worse still, where would I sit? I decided that I wouldn't and retreated.

He ought to be here. None of this felt right.

The steward walked along banging on doors. 'Gold Kaaangarooooo. Dinner's served.'

Gold Kangaroo carriages have beds whereas the Red Kangaroos have chairs that tilt back. I was relieved to be heading for a three-course dinner and not the backpackers' canteen. I would have the luxury of eating on my own so not feel obliged to explain anything to anyone.

It was not to be.

'Ma'am, this way, please. We like to put our single travellers together on one table so it's gonna be a bonzer night for you.'

Early night you mean.

There were three others chatting amiably. I took my place and studied the menu, but there is a limit to how long you can do that so, arranging a smile, I introduced myself. Pleasantries followed, information was gleaned – my company consisted of an English fashion photographer, Peter; a French employee of EDF Energy, Delphine; and an Australian ex-SAS officer-turned-rancher, Harry.

'Can I pour you a glass?' asked Harry. 'It's a great Shiraz from the Barossa Valley.'

I nodded and watched the level rise and wobble with the train's rhythm. I took a sip and looked out of the window. Stars were now slung like Christmas lights across the sky. A different sort of light came into view – a cluster of harsh, incongruous illuminations. I pressed my nose closer to the window.

'It's a prison,' said Harry.

'But it's in the middle of a desert, in the middle of nowhere.'

'Exactly. Nowhere to escape to. They send a lot of illegal immigrants there.' He grinned at my expression. 'They think twice before coming to Australia.'

'Iz a pity we don't 'ave a desert in France,' sighed Delphine.

'Well, desert is what I'm here to photograph,' said Peter. 'Ted Baker fashion on Harleys round Ayers Rock.'

'Good God!' I gasped. 'Another dimension to hot leathers.'

'They wanted me to do the shoot using camels, but they're moodier than the models.'

I thought of Alec Hammersmith and his two-Gs grandpa.

Somehow, during what followed, I ate a three-course meal but each dish got lost among the conversation. I learned of Peter's concern as to how he was going to keep the blowing dust from sticking to sweating models as they posed on Harleys.

'They'll end up looking like the Himba from Namibia,' he complained.

I listened to behind-the-scenes stories from when EDF sponsored the 2007 Rugby World Cup, chuckling at the story involving a job lot of jockstraps. I learned of the perils of ranching in the outback and how, having watched his friends die in Vietnam, Harry was literally spat on by the general public when he got home. I learned to love Shiraz and somewhere in the course of the evening the anxiety and panic of the last months slipped out of my thoughts like coins down the side of a chair.

'I know this is a stupid question, but have you killed anyone?' Yes, stupid, so why ask?

Harry looked at me earnestly. I didn't immediately notice the twinkling eyes.

'Yes,' he replied emphatically. 'Three hundred and fifty-seven – the last three with my bare hands.'

The silence frizzled until, from somewhere quite forgotten, bubbles rose, tracked upwards until they burst out in an explosion of laughter. I couldn't remember the last time I had done that. It proved to be infectious. We all shook and rattled along with the train.

I woke the following morning and gazed out of the window. I stared at the overwhelming vastness of the skies as they seemed to hold down the earth in an immense blue dome.

I had only one thought in my head.

How lucky am I to be doing this?

Debbie Parrott has travelled widely from early childhood. Only over the last few years has she found the time to write articles based on her many travel diaries. In 2015, she was a winner in Bradt's travel-writing competition in the 'best unpublished writer' category. Two stories have been published: one with Bradt and the other in the *Sunday Independent*, but she still struggles to find time to write as she enjoys gathering material far too much.

A January Jaunt to Jordan
Zoe Efstathiou

'You're crazy, going to Jordan on your own.'

I picture my colleague's face when she made that comment, the sidelong look she cast me from behind her monitor, her raised eyebrow and shaking head.

At the time, I'd just shrugged. I hadn't wanted to go to Jordan on my own. I had just got bored one quiet Tuesday night and, in the midst of a restless Googling session, I'd somehow wound up booking a flight leaving in three weeks. *All I need to do is show some initiative, a spirit of adventure, and others will follow*, I'd told myself at the time, assuming that someone would come with me. Someone. But the weeks passed and, strangely enough, no-one leapt at the chance of an out-of-season January jaunt to Jordan.

And so here I am, sitting in an empty, freezing cold dining room at the cheapest hostel in Amman, trying to enjoy a plate of pasta in a peculiar spicy sauce as the man on reception watches me from across the hallway.

I pick up my guidebook, which is lying next to my plate like a talisman, and flick through the pictures – rose-coloured stone, ancient monuments carved in rock, tea lights glittering in front of marbled façades. These are the iconic images of Petra, the otherworldly dreamlike scenes that made me want to come here, and yet right now, in this miserable dining room, I just want to be back in London.

I put the guidebook down. I am crazy, I realise reluctantly, for coming to Jordan on my own. I'm shaking my head, just like my colleague shook hers, when a man appears in the doorway – a Westerner, tall, with a mop of brown curls.

'Ah, hello,' he says, as if he'd been expecting to see me.

'Hi…'

He must be twenty-six or twenty-seven, around my age. He is wearing combats and a faded green jacket, both of which look like they're from an army surplus store.

'I'm Christian. Can I join you?' he asks in a thick Swedish accent, pulling a chair out before I have a chance to respond.

'Sure. I'm Zoe.'

'Cool.' He eyes my pasta and calls over to the man on reception to order a bowl.

He tells me his traveller backstory as we eat. He's from Gothenburg, but took a month off work – IT for a fashion brand – to travel across the Middle East. He's already been to Turkey and Syria, and he's due to visit Iraq and Iran before heading home in two weeks. I can't help feeling impressed. Now *this* is a solo traveller, I think. Bold. Fearless. Enthusiastic. This is the kind of solo traveller I ought to latch myself on to.

'What are you doing tomorrow?' I blurt out. 'I'm thinking of going to Petra. Do you want to come?'

'Sure.' He shrugs. 'That was my plan too,' he tells me, before suggesting we take a local bus rather than the ones offered to tourists because they're a 'tenth of the price'.

The next day, after a night spent in an inhumanly narrow budget bed, I trail after Christian as he hauls a giant camouflage-print backpack on to a rickety old minibus. A compass is hooked to one of the bag's side pockets and a pole is sticking out of the top.

'Is that a tent pole?' I ask.

'It is. I'm going to camp in Petra,' he tells me, matter-of-factly, as he heaves the bag on to the back seat of the bus, which is nothing like the slick air-conditioned ones I'd researched online. Instead, its exterior is flaking with what appears to be a third or fourth layer of paint and the seats have been upholstered with gaffer tape.

'You're camping in Petra? Isn't it... like... locked up at night?'

'Yes, it is, but that's why I brought wire cutters,' Christian tells me, tapping the side of his bag.

'Wire cutters?'

'Yeah.' He unzips a side pocket and pulls out a pair of chunky wire cutters, keeping them lowered behind the seat.

'Oh my god!'

He grins and I can't quite figure out whether he's wildly adventurous or just completely mad.

'So do you camp in UNESCO World Heritage sites often then?'

He laughs. 'Well, there's this competition,' he says, explaining how the company that makes his tent are challenging customers to snap themselves camping in the most unusual and daring place possible in a competition to win 5,000 euros.

'Won't you get arrested though?' I press him. 'Don't they have security?'

'I'm not going until late. The guards will have gone home,' Christian insists.

I nod, still unsure whether he's nuts or not as the bus weaves through the streets of Amman. Eventually the city buildings thin out and parched swathes of desert take over. The bus chugs along isolated roads carved into the barren landscape of lumpy rock. We stop every now and again, the bus drawing to a halt at seemingly unmarked stops to pick up locals, who cast us wary sidelong glances. At Petra, where a small cluster of hotels and restaurants emerges from the desert like a mirage, we lug our bags off the bus and go for dinner, finding a cosy restaurant where we play cards until the sun sets.

Christian looks at his watch. 'Petra's closed now,' he says. 'But I should give it a bit longer just in case.'

He chucks another card on the table and we continue our game.

Half an hour later, we're standing in front of the restaurant.

'So, are you coming then?' Christian asks, gesturing down the darkened road leading to the ancient site.

For a second, I imagine waking up and watching the sun rise over the desert. A once-in-a-lifetime experience. But then I think of the wire cutters, the guards (who I'm not entirely convinced will have all gone home), the cold tent, the danger.

'It's okay... I'm going to the hostel,' I reply, glancing up the street towards the brightly lit tourist bubble. 'Text me if you need a room later. I've got twin beds,' I call after him as he bounds into the darkness.

I settle down in my hostel bedroom, clutching a musty wool blanket. The room is freezing. God knows what it must be like inside Christian's tent, if he's even made it that far. He could be in prison already. I get out my novel and try to unwind while the prayer call echoes over the town. My phone buzzes. Christian.

'Hey, so I set up my tent in Petra but this Bedouin guy came along and told me I'd get arrested... And now I'm staying in his cave! Want to meet us at 6 a.m.? He says he's going to take us on a private tour of Petra.'

What? I reread the text, doing a double take. And I fall asleep feeling a little thrilled about this adventure that has dropped in my lap, simply because I came to Jordan alone in January.

The sky is still dark and cool, shrouded in grey mist, as I enter the twenty-metre high, narrow gorge that leads to the heart of Petra. It's completely silent; apart from the occasional stray cat crossing my path, I'm alone. I feel a twinge in my chest, a swell of wonder and excitement as the mist lifts and the sunlight picks out shades of orange, pink and yellow across the stone walls, the colours marbling into one another. The sun has risen by the time I reach the Treasury, which is instantly recognisable. It is beautiful, majestic and deserted. I head deeper into the ancient town and, after a phone call, find Christian sipping tea, sitting on a tarpaulin spread out in front of a cave.

'Morning,' he calls, his lips twitching as he struggles to suppress a self-satisfied smile.

'So where's your Bedouin friend then?' I ask, sitting down next to him.

Ahmed emerges.

'*Marhaba*,' he says, 'Hello', taking my hand, his eyes distant, misty with sleep. He wears black robes and a long headdress, bound to his head with a white cord, which he sits down and refastens as another Bedouin comes out of the cave.

He looks younger than Ahmed, in his early twenties, and wears a Hawaiian shirt, denim jacket and a green patterned headscarf.

He looks like an eighties rock star. Both of them are in significantly fewer layers than Christian and me but I guess living in a cave come rain or shine toughens you up.

'Hi, I am Masoud,' he says, with a big smile.

'Hi Masoud.' I beam back.

'You want to see the real Petra?' he asks.

'Definitely!' I reply.

We begin our tour, walking deeper into Petra.

'I am from Petra. The sky is my blanket, the earth is my bed,' Masoud tells me, reeling off the line like a lyric he's used many times before; but even so, his eyes sparkle with pride as he delivers it. I wonder, with his flamboyant dress sense, whether he would ever want to leave. With his rough, weather-beaten skin and rotten teeth, he looks wild, too wild for Western life.

He stops to untether a squat donkey. 'And this is Shakira.'

The five of us visit the amphitheatre, palaces, and dozens of caves carved into the desert rock. Ahmed quietly points out things we might otherwise have missed – the faint shadow of a lion carved into a cliff face, irrigation drains carved into the stone – while Masoud chats away, telling us stories about desert life – families with fifteen children, religious ceremonies, goat sacrifices. And then we begin the 850-step ascent to the Monastery, hidden at the peak of a mountain.

'The most beautiful part of Petra, but the hardest to reach,' Masoud says, before letting me ride poor Shakira up the crumbling, well-trodden path. She moves slowly but steadily, pacing out the climb with the well-practised weariness of a donkey used to hauling unfit Westerners up mountains. I suggest getting off, but Masoud insists she's fine.

'Come on, Shakira,' he says, giving her a little slap on the back. She trots a little faster.

'See? Hips don't lie!' he jokes.

Eventually, we reach the Monastery, a smooth, classically pillared façade carved into a pitted peak of rock. It stands tall and ornate, in stark contrast to the unruly landscape below, where misshapen mounds, like the sloppy sandcastles I made as a child, emerge from the dry expanse.

Masoud greets a woman sitting on a blanket by the entrance, with a giant curved black teapot in front of her, no doubt waiting to sell tea to tourists.

'This is Fatima,' he says.

'Marhaba, marhaba, hi,' Fatima greets us, as she pours the tea into small glasses and gestures for us to sit down.

Her husband comes out of a nearby cave, a small-boned man with dirt caught in his wrinkles. She hands him cups of tea to pass around. Masoud pets Shakira while Ahmed gazes towards the desert, his headscarf billowing on the breeze. Christian takes photographs. I take a steaming cup, nodding thanks to Fatima, who smiles back. I look out over the desert, an endless shade of rosy orange like nothing I've ever seen before. I take a sip, relishing the warm, incredibly sweet liquid, and suddenly I don't feel so crazy to have come to Jordan on my own, after all.

I may not be the most intrepid solo traveller and I certainly don't carry around a compass or wire cutters, but I don't need that stuff. In fact, all anyone really needs when they're travelling alone is to be open – open to new people and new adventures – because when you are that way, being a solo traveller really isn't very solo at all.

'Cheers,' I say to Christian, tapping my glass against his.

Zoe Efstathiou is a journalist for the *Daily Express*, where she covers national and world news and reviews commercial women's fiction. She adores writing and is currently editing her first novel – a romantic comedy set in London. When she  isn't writing, Zoe enjoys painting, walking her dog, going to the theatre and daydreaming about her next getaway.

Taxi Ride in Vladivostok

Nicole Teufel

It was the country that terrified every American for a generation: Russia. Full of slick, conniving bastards who were a threat to our way of life. It seems an attitude from years ago, but every teacher, professor, parent and neighbour had a suspicion of Russians, a very real fear. Part of me learned to subconsciously dislike this country for as long as I could remember. Even if I was never taught to hide under a desk I was still left with a subconscious disdain for Russia – or rather Russians. Not just their politicians and their system of government, but Russians themselves. It still felt patriotic to root against them, even in trivial competitions. It felt natural to distrust them. The Cold War was over and I was never alive for it, yet somehow I still managed to have a bad taste in my mouth for a group of people of whom I had never met a single one. So that is precisely why I had to go there. I had to see what it was all about.

The only thing I really knew about Russia was that it was big. So to grasp that enormous scale, I was going to have to take at least six weeks to explore it. I wanted to do the Trans-Siberian Railway because it sounded romantic and majestic. It also seemed like the kind of thing that was on everyone's bucket list but which no-one ever actually did. The kind of thing that was scarier to not do than to do, because you knew if you didn't do it now, you'd wake up wondering where all the time went as you tried to carve out even a single free weekend for yourself. But not everyone thinks like this and there was no one who could travel with me for so long. Yet could I really go all alone, at only eighteen? Already I had packed up and moved to Japan on my own after graduating high school, so I knew my parents would need little persuading, especially since I was funding everything myself, but I still needed to be convinced that I could indeed do this on my own. There I was, a young single girl who'd never travelled alone before, but who wasn't going to give up this opportunity out of fear.

So I bought a Siberian Airlines ticket to Vladivostok in time for the thaw of spring and before I knew it I was showing my visa to a Russian customs agent and trudging through the tiny airport with all that I thought I needed for the long trip in a single bag. And then it hit me. What was I doing here? I was ten thousand kilometres from home, a thousand kilometres from my school and all of my friends, and fifty kilometres away from the hostel I had booked for that night.

I arrived trying to suppress my unconscious negativity towards Russians, but a minute in I had already failed. A man came up to me wearing a sign saying he was a taxi driver. I immediately told him no. He had the same cold face of every terrorist and kidnapper I was ever warned about from movies and television shows. I tried to find the bus I had read about, but I was very lost and so when he offered again I said yes. The more confused I looked, I thought, the more vulnerable I was and it was time for a decision. As my heart raced, I followed him out and I heard every relative and friend of mine telling me to turn back.

I was so stupid and this was why I shouldn't have come. I checked to see if it was a marked cab. It was, and the other drivers knew him and even let out a greeting as he passed. There wasn't a single reason not to trust him, but I was still on edge. I got in and waited to be driven to some far-off place and never be heard from again.

Then he was on the phone – telling his friends, I was sure, that he had tricked a stupid foreigner. He started talking to me, yelling about something and pointing to the door. I rolled down the window. That was wrong. He pointed again and I looked down. A tourist map and brochures. I looked through them. You would think at this point I'd be over my irrational fear, but I was still convinced that this was all a ploy to trick me and that he was still planning on robbing me or worse. Then he started talking again, and he asked if I spoke English. I said yes and he began yelling into his phone's translator. He showed me the word: 'present'. I assumed he wanted the money now – the only logical explanation – and handed him 2,000 rubles. He waved me away and pointed. Now I got it. The brochures were for me to keep.

His next translation was 'low-water bridge', and boy, was there a low-water bridge. The bridge was so close to the water we were almost gliding on top of it and I was able to look across the bay at the sunset. He rolled the window down so I could take a good photo. It was my first glimpse of the beauty I would continue to encounter in the most unexpected places here. Then he started pointing to the right and saying some words in Russian that I couldn't understand. I thought that must be where he was going to pull over and lead me to my death, now that he had my trust. But no, he rolled the window down again so I could take a picture of what he had been pointing to – a monastery.

We passed under a large crest and he motioned with his hands and said 'Vladivostok'. We were now in the city and the crest of a tiger, he explained, was its symbol. At this time, the taxi driver introduced himself as Alexander and asked me my name. As we passed various places he would say, 'Nicole, Nicole,' and point to the best photo spots. He turned around in his seat and opened the map I had, pointing out the sights. We soon neared a spot marked with a camera and he yelled at me, 'Photo! Photo!' I saw the most incredible view of the Golden Horn Bridge, Vladivostok's new marvel spanning the bay. I suddenly felt embarrassed and a little ashamed. He was the kindest cab driver I'd ever known. And yet I had taken him to be a crook. I had a lot to learn.

This was why I had come to Russia. All I knew about it was that it was evil and full of communists. We had barely touched Russian history during high school and when we did it was to compare Russia to America and declare that we were superior. In fact, a classmate had told me that Vladivostok was a desolate city, so awful the Russians had to pay people to live there. That's what had motivated me to make sure it was a part of my trip.

The driver pointed to a large clock. 'Big Ben,' he joked.

We arrived at the hostel and I gave him a tip and a smile. I wasn't expecting him to get out of the car and walk me to the door. It was a large and imposing building; there were no signs and you needed a mysterious code to get in. Once we got in, rushing through the door as someone exited, he asked passers-by where the hostel was. Eventually he asked me if I had contact information and when I showed him the phone number, he called them for me and they told him a worker would come and get me if I waited where I was. They soon came while Alexander was moving his car out of the way of traffic. I didn't get to say goodbye or thank you to the man whose kindness would set the tone for my trip and forever change my view of the Russian people. Without him I would still be waiting outside that building, trying to find my bed for the night.

Instead, I got into the hostel, unpacked the very little I had into a locker, and fell asleep thinking about the weeks to come.

Nicole Teufel is a nineteen-year-old university student from Pennsylvania who lives in Tokyo, Japan. Apart from Russia she has travelled in France, Belgium, Ireland, Canada, Germany and China.

Tips

Most tourists are just as friendly as you are, but sometimes you need to make the first move. *Ian Douglas*

Dismissing everyone as a would-be amour or opportunist has almost cost me a few worthwhile relationships. Try to be open-minded. *Claire Davies*

Although you will feel as though you are unique in travelling alone, you will find this is far from the case. If still feeling a bit undecided about taking the plunge, remind yourself of how lucky you are to be in the position to choose such a trip. Go for it! *Christine Green*

When I travelled solo in South America many years ago I brought a sketchbook and soft pencils and did portraits of children, which I then gave to them. It was so much more interactive than taking photos and the kids – and their parents – loved it. *Hilary Bradt*

Traveller credit cards, such as Revolut, allow you to stay in control of your money and exchange rates. *Matt Dawson*

Face the Fear

✦ ✦ ✦

Facing the fear is the nub of this book and the focus of this chapter. If you tend to think of women as the nervous travellers, Ian Oliver's admission of his multiple anxieties is particularly refreshing. Sometimes the key moment is to choose, as Kelly Dignan does, whether 'I rule fear or it rules me'. Hannah Stuart-Leach forces herself out of her comfort zone to work as volunteer in the Philippines. And finally there is no happy ending to a story about being ripped off on a challenging solo trip to Nepal – except that Claire Davies emerges from it safely, and acknowledges that in spite of the difficulties, 'for some reason, in the years that followed, I was drawn again to travelling alone... I've become addicted to the other things that solitary travel brings. Being alone sharpens the senses and, therefore, heightens the experience.'

Darkness in Laos
Ian Oliver

Click.

The room plunged into darkness. The whirring of the overhead fan slowed gradually before coming to a complete stop. From the distance came a short, raucous cheer before silence descended; the only sound now penetrating the still, heavy night air was the distinctive chirruping of crickets, the stereotypical tropical background noise.

Had you asked me last week, I'd have said that this was one of those situations that might have sent me into a downward spiral of self-doubt and homesickness – being stuck in a foreign country, not knowing anyone, not being able to speak the language and not being able to ask simple questions like, 'When is the power coming back on?' – but for some reason all I did was lie on my bed and think about how things had changed over the last few days with a relaxed, resigned, smile on my face.

I'm a bit of a control-freak. I always need to know what's happening at any given time, and don't like being left in the dark, as it were. My mantra is 'knowledge is power,' so before I left on my trip I did a lot of research – everything from cultural norms (always use your right hand) to learning numbers and polite greetings (although, as a typical Brit, foreign languages stay in my head for approximately thirty-five seconds), even down to making notes about which bus goes where, how much it costs and whether I pay on entry or just pass the money down the bus once I've sat down. I knew therefore that there was no sense in getting stressed in my hotel room about a mere power cut. Here in Laos (Please Don't Rush – the unofficial nickname for the LDPR or Lao People's Democratic Republic) I'd read that things happened. You just had to wait for them to pass.

This was partly why I'd chosen to come to Laos in the first place. A couple of months previously, my manager at work had reminded me that I still had a lot of annual leave I needed to take before the end of the financial year. I wanted to do something interesting with it as it seemed a waste to spend it all at home in bed. I'd always been interested in travel, but most of my solo trips abroad had been either to visit people I knew already or to places where I was comfortable with the language and culture. On the rare occasions I'd travelled somewhere different, I'd gone with a friend.

My last major solo trip to a non-English-speaking destination had been a complete disaster. Exactly ten years previously I'd gone to Italy. It was not long after a relationship breakup and I'd really not been in the right place mentally, as a result of which all my paranoid fears and introverted panics about being alone in a foreign culture had surfaced. I virtually didn't eat because I was too scared to order food in a café, quickly realised I couldn't cope and ultimately came back home a week early. I was desperate to make sure that the same thing didn't happen again.

I'd asked around my travel-oriented friends and also online. I needed somewhere 'easy' for a first-time backpacker – a place where I could get around without too much problem, where I could be understood easily and where I'd be around other backpackers if I needed help, yet was also different enough from home to be interesting. It also needed to be a reasonably inexpensive destination. Without fail, they all said the same thing – southeast Asia. They said it was an easy place to explore as a solo traveller, as no matter where I went there would always be other backpackers, but that there was so much there to see and do that I wouldn't get bored, and if I wanted to find my own space it would be very easy to go somewhere out of the way.

While reading guidebooks and online forums, I made copious notes, listed places that seemed interesting and learned how to get to them. I planned out different itineraries, so that at any given town I'd have two or three alternative onward routings. I knew that if anything went wrong, I'd still be 'on plan', although I then started to worry that I was overthinking a little.

The closer my departure date got, the more I fretted. I had tried to book a couple of hotels and some travel tickets in advance, but the transactions had failed. My bank didn't seem to like me using my debit card for purchases in Malaysia. I started to worry that money would end up being a problem. A few years before I'd got into a lot of debt and so only possessed one bank debit card and no credit cards. I would be reliant on that card, and any cash I took with me, to get me through the trip.

As I'd not done anything like this for a long time, and I'm one of those people who always imagines the worst possible scenarios, I created other disasters in my head every time I thought about it. What if I couldn't get to the right bus station? What if I needed to ask someone how to reach a place and found they didn't speak my language? What if everyone laughed at me because I got the pronunciation of a word wrong and said something rude – for all I knew, the Khmer word for 'penis' was a single tone away from their word for 'rice'. I really don't like being the centre of attention, and

I certainly wouldn't enjoy being the odd one out, the ignorant *falang* to be stared at and made fun of.

When the day for departure came, all manner of little things went wrong. The friend I was going to couchsurf with in Sheffield bailed on me at the last minute so I had to find a hotel for the night. Something went wrong with my phone and it suddenly refused to start charging, which meant among other things I no longer had a suitable alarm clock. The entertainment system on my first outbound flight kept crashing, and it was almost impossible to connect to any of the free Wi-Fi spots en route. While none of these problems were of major significance, they heightened my feelings of fear and pessimism. The closer I got to landing in Kuala Lumpur – where I'd booked a two-night stopover in a guesthouse before my flight to Laos – the more my stomach churned, the more my mind came up with fanciful reasons why I'd end up staying in my room all day and not be brave enough to come out.

And yet.

My arrival in Kuala Lumpur Airport was a breeze. I had no problem getting local currency, and catching the bus into the city centre proved uncomplicated. Negotiating the local metro network and buying tickets, despite the crowded station where I felt any mistake would be highlighted and mocked, was also much easier than I'd anticipated, while the city itself was far simpler to navigate for a first-time traveller than I'd feared.

This gave me confidence for my next step, the trip to Laos. True, it would be a step into the unknown, but somehow, having already negotiated Malaysia, I felt more secure that things were going to be all right. And indeed I experienced fewer negative thoughts on that early morning two-hour flight to Vientiane. My fears hadn't dissipated completely; I spent the whole night beforehand worrying about the change of scenery, about my phone dying and not waking me up, so that I hardly slept, but at least I was improving.

The ultimate test was a little episode in Vientiane Bus Station, which I passed with flying colours. I'd noted that nearby was 'Buddha Park', a weird garden laid out by an eccentric millionaire. A direct local bus went there, but the standard practice among Western backpackers was to catch a taxi. I'd made a note of which bus to catch and, while it would have been easy for me to give in to the catcalls of the taxi drivers, I made sure I caught it. This may sound like a small thing, but only a couple of months before the idea of negotiating a bus station in a foreign country with an alien language would have been a hard limit for me.

And so here I was, in a guesthouse in Vientiane, during a power cut of indeterminate length, not knowing what was going on, not able to speak the language to ask, yet not being fazed by any of it. I was learning, in stages, what I was capable of, and challenging my limits, and it was honestly good fun. I had many challenges left, of course, but at least I knew I wasn't going to crawl under a duvet at the first sign of trouble. I had finally beaten my ten-year Italian bugbear.

Ian Oliver is a budget backpacker from northern England with a preference for unusual destinations, dark history, abandoned places, street art and not wearing shoes. If not getting squashed on local minibuses, he can be found in micropubs drinking beer he's never heard of, or taking his camera on long random walks.

Unenlightened in Nepal
Claire Davies

The narrow wooden boat cut through the glassy surface of Lake Phewa in the Pokhara valley, the boatman a silhouette at the prow in the diminutive shape of the Nepalese. So far the local people had lived up to their reputation for being kind and gentle. Around the lake, the lower slopes of the mountains threw a dark reflection on to the evening waters; but the upper peaks remained elusive, shrouded in monsoon clouds. I had yet to visualise the Himalayas – the aim of this trip, my first outside Europe and travelling alone. I had agreed with the boatman to an hour on the lake for a fee of 600 rupees, half payable in advance and half on return, in the hope that the sunset would briefly illuminate the mountains. Somehow, various things had not gone to plan.

Suddenly the boatman ceased his work of creating spools of ripples with his oar and lit a cigarette. Smoke plumed up, the smell of cheap nicotine polluting the mountain air washed clean of dust by the afternoon rain. This was supposed to be one of my solo traveller moments. Here, in the middle of Lake Phewa at sunset, I could have had all the clichés. I would be clearer about myself, think of a new career or perhaps even find a new religion. I would be like the traveller I had passed on the lakeshore, sitting cross-legged meditating in the terraced fields. This was supposed to be it. Perhaps the boatman would share stories about his struggles as a Tibetan refugee or tales of bravery and loss as a Sherpa. So far, however, he had proven to be a sullen character and now he was about to turn around and convey his own ideas about our little evening sojourn.

'You give me six hundred rupees again or no go back.' He gestured towards the shore, his arm as thin as the oar handle but, I suspected, extremely strong.

We floated for a few minutes, almost immobile on the vast sheet of water, the boat seeming to bob only with my breath. I shook my head to indicate my refusal, but the boatman simply lit another cigarette, flicking ash on to the water where it floated, briefly, before slowly dispersing, swallowed by the waters which were turning black with the disappearing light. Sunset itself had been a bit of a washout on account of the low clouds. Dusk was now a serious entity, the green of the lower mountain slopes taking on grey hues. I eyed the boatman's boy, hoping to appeal to his sense of justice, but he had the same scavenging look as the boatman.

A little bit of colonial Britain rose up arrogantly inside of me. Surely they couldn't do this to me? Wouldn't justice ultimately prevail? But as the fingers of cold from the mountains crept over the lake, chilling the wooden bench below me, I began to feel afraid.

What would other solo travellers do? Maybe they would try and negotiate with the surly boatman, befriend him or find out the story of hardship that had driven him to this. Or perhaps they would sit it out in the darkness at an impasse until the boatman gave in and rowed home. Swimming to shore was another option, but we had rowed out for half an hour and I didn't fancy it; besides I was increasingly conscious of my money belt which I carried on me at all times and checked regularly with paranoia. The only reassurance was that a physical tussle with the boatman was likely to find all of us in the water, although I was now also wondering who or what else might be waiting for us back at shore.

Things were not really working out for my first solo trip.

I had come here thinking it was time for an adventure. As a young woman, I had arrived at a fairly prestigious medical school, straight out of my northern comprehensive, to find that many other students had been to public school and had moneyed parents who had sent them on a gap year – at the time an unknown concept in my home town of Middlesbrough – or else they took off to Thailand or Indonesia for the summer holidays. I had walked on Kashmiri carpets in student bedrooms and listened to the lament of someone who had been forced to spend their first six months as a medical student teetotal on account of a bad case of hepatitis A. But as well as the hardcore adventures, people had also had 'experiences', exciting love affairs and the like, or had overcome past traumas. 'You meet such fascinating people,' one of my friends had said.

And so, here I was, alone in Nepal for two weeks. So far, I rated my enjoyment as neutral.

I was having a lot of the wrong sort of experiences with the wrong kind of people. In Kathmandu, dogs had howled all night outside my hotel. Someone had persuaded me to move into an ashram which cost one pound a night, but I had woken up with two cockroaches the size of saucers on my face. Looking lost and tired in Durbar Square, I was picked up by two female hippies who took me to a Tibetan restaurant in Freak Street and then back to their cell-like room with layer upon layer of graffiti on the walls. The girls had proceeded to skin up and get stoned, which alarmed me – some of the restaurants had noticeboards featuring small advertisements suggesting people might like to visit various foreigners imprisoned on drug charges. One of the hippies related her story of bloody diarrhoea – probably amoebic dysentery – which she was trying, and failing, to treat naturally. I tried not to show that this offended my medical sensibilities, particularly as we had just shared a bowl of Tibetan dumpling soup.

Most evenings in Pokhara, I had found myself in the company of a young woman from Cornwall, ostensibly normal, but on fire with activism. Every night I listened to monologues on the Israeli question, the Irish question, the Tibetan question and whatever else she considered was wrong with the world.

Everyone else seemed to have been travelling for months, if not years – mainly in India, which they pronounced 'Indiyah' – raising eyebrows at my two-week holiday as it emerged that I just didn't speak the language of travellers: spirituality, Varanasi, 'roops' for rupees, long bus journeys and tales of diarrhoea. I had no illness stories to share and was unlikely to accumulate any. My medical background had gone into overdrive trying to avoid illnesses. I spurned salads, refused to put my toothbrush in the tap water, pulled my meals apart to ensure I only ate things that were cooked through and was sticky from insect repellent. While other people were reading Rainer Maria Rilke and Hermann Hesse, I usually had my nose in the guidebook revising how best to avoid germs.

Back on the lake, I watched the light dim and the mountain slopes become shapes. The darkness of the water made it look ominously deeper. Cold ran across my bare arms. The boat rocked gently like a cradle as the three of us sat there in silence, a sullen little trio, each of us waiting for someone to crack. The boatman was now simply a glowing cigarette, the tip like a fleck of lava in the dark.

The boat boy perched at the helm, bare toes curled over the woodwork, seemingly immune to the cold.

I finally realised there were going to be no heroic endings, no twists to the tale to write home about, no changes to the atmosphere or extensions of the international hand of friendship. I was being ripped off, good and proper. With night upon us, I was also increasingly afraid. My family knew I was in Pokhara, but that was it: no-one knew I had taken a boat out or even which hotel I was in. I remembered another poster in Kathmandu about a young man who had mysteriously disappeared. I had put it down to drugs at the time, but now I saw how easily it could happen. As I indicated wearily that I was paying up, the boatman began the long paddle back to shore.

Relief flooded over me as I felt the prow connect with solid ground. The boatman then attempted to extract more money from me for the extra time on the lake. This time, being back on land, I shouted at him and it seemed to do the trick. I stumbled up towards the distant lights, over the rough, terraced fields, now dark and devoid of meditators, the smell of wood smoke from some old shacks guiding my way ahead.

The rest of the trip continued in a similar vein. I kept meeting the wrong people in the wrong places and continually found myself being thwarted in my quests. The Himalayas remained hidden behind cloud apart from five minutes very early one morning when the sunrise illuminated the peaks pink and white like a vast ridge of Turkish Delight. There was no spiritual revelation, no sense of enlightenment. When I flew back, there was no career change. On the plus side, my fastidious habits paid off and there was also no amoebic dysentery or hepatitis A.

But for some reason, in the years that followed, I was drawn again to travelling alone. Further trips took me to Thailand, Burma, India, Greece and Spain. Even as I write this, I am alone in Ethiopia. Travelling alone is difficult. I get lonely. The attention from people, especially men, can be annoying and sometimes I'm afraid. But I've become addicted to the other things that solitary travel brings. Being alone sharpens the senses and, therefore, heightens the experience. Views, sounds, people – everything swings into focus when I am free of the distractions of other individuals. A travelling companion brings company, but also the need to negotiate how you spend each other's time, support each other and tolerate each other's moans.

Now I am married, I notice how I become less visible in certain countries when with my husband. In Ethiopia, people communicate through him – as a mark of respect perhaps – but it gets boring sitting in the back of a taxi hearing, 'And what about her?' yet again. Being alone has always brought me richer relationships and revealed tantalising snippets of life – whispered conversations about politics in Myanmar, stories of migrants' thwarted attempts to cross the Mediterranean, the confessions of a people trafficker and the painful memories of Ethiopia's Derg.

Being alone is hard. I have despaired of many things, but I'm also addicted to that feeling when, as the plane takes off, I'm away from real life, suspended above it all, with new adventures, new stories and new relationships ahead. I never did find that elusive new career, start my own NGO or write a book, but I still seek out the moments that only being alone can bring, not hoping it will change my life.

Claire Davies finally made it through medical school and is now a doctor and freelance writer in east London. When not working, she can be found gardening, cycling or doing yoga. She can speak three words of Amharic, which is enough to surprise  most Ethiopians, and a little bit more French. She does not like cooking and leaves this to her husband. Her website is at www.drclairedavies.com.

Tea and Oranges

Kelly Dignan

'The devil is a lion with no teeth.'

This I read in a café in Algeciras, Spain, that served English breakfasts and kept notebooks that travellers wrote in upon return from Tangier, just across the water in Morocco. With warnings of sickness and scams, lopsided flowers drawn beside declarations that one only had to 'let go and go', the notebooks were both fuelling my anxiety and spurring me on. I'd been delaying getting on the ferry since I arrived two days earlier and now felt dizzy, drowning in humidity and all the more doubtful about going to Morocco on my own.

As I'd made my way down to the bottom of Spain from Barcelona, everyone who heard my plan thought I was being reckless, that I should wait until I had a friend, preferably a man, to make the trip with me. One traveller said going there on my own was akin to throwing myself into a lion's den, that I'd be preyed upon the whole time. I had an image of myself fending off harassment and unwanted attention with a metaphorical stick, unable to enjoy the experience without constantly looking over my shoulder. I left the café to look for a faux wedding ring and bottle of Imodium, figuring I'd see how I felt in the morning. If I still could not get on the boat, it would be time to take a train back north.

I had an awful night of nervous nightmares. Out in the silhouettes of Algeciras's eerie steeples was the endless, unnatural shrieking of an animal. I got up long before a cock was crowing and went down to the docks where fog rose up from the sea beneath stagnant palm trees. The city sounded, even in its sleep, as though it was hissing.

I sat by the port imagining all that might go wrong in Morocco, watching the clock. The Rock of Gibraltar rose up before me and would stand as solidly no matter what I chose to do. I felt as if I was in the midst of a half-read novel, and that however the next few weeks turned out would just be what the story was, as if it was already written. There was the version where I got on the boat for Tangier, and the version where I baulked and headed back up into Spain. This is the moment, I said to myself, where I rule fear or it rules me.

I got on the boat for Tangier.

Rocking across the strait, the ferry was empty except for a rowdy group of Spanish couples and lone men strolling through the tiny duty free. One of the crew came over to the railing where I stood watching the waves, surprised I was going to Morocco on my own. He wrote out names and numbers of family members in Casablanca, then brought me to an abandoned dining room and with absurd formality un-looped napkins and upturned cups, serving me a free breakfast as soon I would not be able to eat until sundown. Out of the window, the white hillsides of Tangier came into view.

I huddled around the Spanish group as hands hitched rope and attached the boat to northern Africa. I could see the glassy terminal and, sure enough, a cluster of men waiting around the entrance. I tried to melt myself to invisibility as we came through the gates but was left alone, becoming disorientated, and the pack set upon me in a swarm, shouting, '*Vous cherchez quelque chose, mademoiselle?*' and '*Hola*

Coca-Cola!' and 'Don't worry, it's Ramadan,' as I stepped into a city lit with rain, the tumbling white buildings aglow. Wailing crackled the air, the call to prayer vibrating the technicolour puddles. I got into a *petit taxi* that drove through illuminated architecture and picked men up along the way; they chatted in Arabic and politely pretended I wasn't there. The driver dropped me at the bus terminal, slipping me a piece of paper with his phone number, saying that when I came back he would take me out to the mountains where he and his friends played guitars, and he sang 'Lady Madonna' as I paid him.

I boarded a falling-apart bus to Chefchaouen, a small village in the Rif Mountains where I wanted to go to because of pictures I'd seen of the medina, painted only in various shades of blue. I constructed Morocco by what I saw out of the window – straw huts, goats and overburdened donkeys, shacks of nothing but bulbous onions, men leaning against trees in empty expanses, mud roads and spots of villages, chickens slung like guns by the feet, kids lying down in a field or throwing stones at scraggy sheep, houses with open-air windows and rooftops of strung-out laundry, women descending long disconnected stairs barefoot. Half-turned heads watched us pass dust through their daily lives. Around me men fell into the aisle, grabbing each other at the shoulders, carrying on in unburst bubbles of debate.

We arrived in huge drops of rain. I made the steep climb into Chefchaouen, soaking my map, all the while people appearing like apparitions, asking if I needed any help. I found a hotel and took a windowless room with only a bed and a prayer mat. Two Japanese guys were across the hall and took me under their wing. We went up puddled steps to the rooftop, the white squares of its chequered floor glowing under moonlight, and looked down on the village radiant blue, the spectres of mountains floating around the flooded mud of the town. Squat houses were all decorated from the same palette, like shades of the sky at different times of the day, and everything was quietening down, as if on pause, as lights flickered out in windows.

When we came back in, the power in the hotel seemed to have been cut as well. Taka consulted a complex grid taped to the wall, put his hands together. 'They are reciting the Koran.' We listened on the stairs until a siren spun, and then went down to a room full of men singing and eating. We ordered *tagine* and during the hour it took to make, men revolved playing pool, smoking, and looking at me. Yoshi and I traded seats so my back was to the room, but stares lurched from under umbrellas and leers came from the café across the way. I felt like a stranded animal and wondered how I would explore the streets beyond the safety of the hotel, but I focused on talking about Tokyo, listening to the drumbeat of the rain, and taking things moment by moment. Our food was set down in earthen pots, next to a basket of bread, and the man who had cooked for us peeked out from the kitchen, watching us eat.

Two locals glided up to us, one with an impressive moustache, visiting from the nearby mountains. We made conversation as if through a sieve – Arabic was translated into French that I relayed in English and which was then discussed in Japanese. Mustafa recited proverbs and I thought about how everywhere, from the bar stools of the small town where I am from, across oceans and through misted mountains, to pale blue villages beneath inverted stars, people were gathered in rooms talking about living and how to live. The man with the moustache kept interrupting and Mustafa told me he was proposing marriage with an offering of camels.

A woman in slippers scraped into the room with a tray of mint tea, sweet and steaming in long glasses, stuffed with rough leaves, and a bowl of tangerines. I remembered the crate of tangerines in my kitchen in Montreal where I would drink tea on Saturday mornings listening to African music on the radio, as if that moment contained in itself a premonition of here, a day when I would pass into northern Africa and eat a tangerine above the smell of sundown and feasting out in the street. And in the same way I foresaw from the room where Mustafa scribbled memorised verses into my notebook ('We come spinning out of nothingness, scattering stars like dust...') to a time long after I left Morocco when I would live in a city still unknown to me and, peeling a tangerine, thumbing the Maroc sticker on to the fridge, or listening to that Leonard Cohen song with the line about tea and oranges, I would remember this moment, a day I tumbled into a new jumble of geometries and spices in the air, transported to what felt like a whole new world, because I was not afraid.

Mustafa escorted me out into the lit-up labyrinth of Chefchaouen. Displays of saffron and stacks of dates, pomegranates, gorgeous old archways, cats curled in corners and rooster coops. Sun-stained muscles stretched and pressed leather, in front of which a shopkeeper ducked under purses and spread out his hands. A heap of shoes waited outside a mosque where bodies touched foreheads to carpet and prayed. Chickpea stands and smoking grills curled calligraphy on to the sky, mingling with the snaking smoke of a packed café where a den of men watched *Gladiator* on a tiny television, holding silver pots in the air, steaming mint tea.

All through the medina pale blue gave way to paler blue, powder blue, turquoise. I felt as if we were wandering through an ancient ice cave, enclosed in pure blue shards of walls, frozen in time, or timeless, passing through night in a village that seemed like it could have just as easily been centuries in the past or into the future.

At the edge of the Ville Nouvelle we came to the cascades, black waterfalls rumbling down the mountain, and in the squares of light that scattered from Chefchaouen on to the water I saw the dots that dashed through the drape of the night train I took back to Tangier after several weeks of breaking bread at sunset and watching moons reflect on minarets and being helped all along the way by the kindness of strangers. All that night I would be pensive as we traversed the coast, thinking about how I suddenly felt I could take on anything, that abstract shadows and the unknown would no longer scare me, carefully placing all I had learned in Morocco, from hunger to haggling, into a perfect shape, a delicate shape, like a pyramid of oranges.

Kelly Dignan is a Toronto writer whose passion for travel has taken her to fifty-five countries around the world. Recently she spent three years in Shanghai working for Ctrip, China's largest travel company. She has published pieces in *Away*, *Bamboo Compass* and *The Globe & Mail*. Currently she lives in Kuala Lumpur.

Finding Freedom
Hannah Stuart-Leach

I've always been an anxious sort of person. I assumed it had developed over time, but my mother recently assured me that even as a toddler, I was terrified of snow – which means I must have been anxious from day one as it was snowing the day I was born.

Then, as an older child, I would happily sacrifice my own sister if we came face to face with a dog on the way home from school.

I've come to accept that worrying is part of who I am. But that doesn't mean I'm going to let it stop me doing things. In fact, quite the opposite. The only way I've found to combat anxiety is – as self-help gurus so carelessly advise – to feel the fear and do it anyway.

This is how nine years ago I found myself ending a comfortable, but not-quite-right, relationship; how I left a stable, but uninspiring, job in London; and how I took a job as an English teacher, on the other side of the world, in South Korea.

I was so terrified at the prospect of the long-haul flight on a Korean airline – which historically suffered a slightly dodgy reputation – that I turned down the *free* journey, paid for by the school, and booked my own flight. I definitely felt my fears, and they cost me 600 pounds.

Although moving to South Korea sounds like a big step – and it was – it was still a relatively safe set-up. I lived with a great group of American, Canadian and English teachers and each weekend we headed out to explore Korea together. It was like being a student again, and much easier than my almost-adult life in the UK had been. During holidays and in between contracts I even went off to see more of Asia: Thailand, Laos, Cambodia, Indonesia, Taiwan. But I was always with someone else, and could share the stresses of strange lands.

Then one day, a bit fed up and bored during a lunch break at school, I checked my horoscope. 'Travel, or taking on a new lifestyle or interest, will do you good,' it said. Pretty standard. But it went on, 'A change may be required in order to fulfil a dream.' And then, to my great annoyance, I experienced a familiar nagging feeling in the pit of my stomach – it was time for a new adventure. Except this time, on my own.

I decided on a month-long volunteer programme in the Philippines, as an antidote to the very wealthy *hagwon*, or private school, I'd been working at in South Korea. It had started to seem a bit much, seeing three-year-old tots coming to school dressed head to toe in Burberry, their little lunchboxes concealed inside leather briefcases, and I wanted to help people less privileged.

Part of my anxiously inclined mind is determined to catastrophise, however, so the idea of the Philippines, at the time constantly in the news for its plane crashes, boat sinkings and natural disasters, was one big nightmare for me. Maybe subconsciously, that's why I chose it. I knew it was a challenge. But, like many anxious people, I'm my own worst enemy. I combed the FCO's travel advice, always overly alarming, and researched all the possible disasters that could occur and every hideous illness I could conceivably contract. Japanese encephalitis was a big one, where your brain oozes out of your ears. Despite the one-in-a-million odds, I wasn't placated. All it takes is one mosquito bite, and if anyone's going to get that mosquito bite, it's bound to be me.

I managed to find a volunteer programme with a craft group, the Payawpao Orchids, who made all sorts of accessories out of recycled paper. With unemployment around 85 per cent in the village, many men left for the cities. Extra income, earned in a flexible way like this, was a lifeline for the women left behind. It was on Tablas, the largest of the Romblon islands, and the only way to reach it was by a twelve-hour overnight ferry. Just the thought made me seasick.

I boarded the ferry like a condemned woman, my heart thudding against my chest, palms clammy and clenched, looking up at the sky and analysing the colour and form of the clouds for signs of a storm.

It was just as chaotic as I'd imagined: women getting on with boxes of roosters, kids running around screaming, people and belongings sprawled all over the deck. To make matters worse, the captain was drunk. After a short time, just as rumblings of a storm started to rock the boat, he passed out on a bench with a can of San Miguel by his side.

I sat cross-legged on a plastic-covered bunk bed, barely moving or muttering a word. My diary entry from that long, long night on the top deck, half-exposed to the wind and rain, is jittery and rambling. I can still feel the nervous energy just looking at those frantic scrawlings. But there's also a certain self-awareness: 'At twenty seven I am finally brave enough to do this kind of thing, I think when I am alone I have more strength. If I'm with other people, I rely on them for reassurance, but alone I can't do that, and if I am scared, I have no choice but to get on with it… I am coming to accept that I needed this.'

Then, as the movement of the boat reduced to a gentle sway, I got up off my bunk and stood against the railing to watch my first moonrise. A magnificent, hopeful sight in the black of the night, in the middle of the ocean. And in a light, carefree cursive, as if I'm still not quite convinced but trying to persuade myself, I wrote in Filipino: '*Bahala na*,' meaning, 'What will be, will be.'

Just as dawn broke I arrived in Sogod where I'd be staying. It looked to me as wild as a scene from the television series *Lost*, with bamboo shacks hiding amid the palm trees. I could smell fires burning, ready for breakfast, and was surprised to see most of the villagers already up.

Another volunteer, Philip, from the Netherlands, welcomed me on to my host family's porch and offered me a cup of sugary instant coffee and a strong cigarette. Despite being overtired and over-stoked on caffeine and adrenaline – not the best combination for an anxious soul – I knew instantly I was in the right place.

After lots of happy hellos, I went to dump my stuff in my bedroom. There was a bed with a scraggy mosquito net overhead; a lizard on the wall, looking nonplussed; and this Joseph Addison quote painted on to a piece of wood: 'What sunshine is to flowers, smiles are to humanity. These are but trifles, to be sure; but scattered along life's pathway, the good they do is inconceivable.'

One of the loveliest things about volunteering was staying with a local family – Ma Tess, her husband Felix and various children and volunteers. Ma Tess was a school teacher, larger than life and very much the village matriarch. She could usually be heard exclaiming 'Arrrrooy!' – the Filipino for 'Wow!' – with an almighty rolling of 'r's, while gossiping with passing neighbours, her expressive lips pointing in the general direction of whomever they happened to be discussing. Meanwhile Felix, a portly chap with a marvellous moustache, could often be found doling out Ma Tess's prescriptions of 80-per-cent-proof gin to anyone with the slightest sniffle, or chilling out in his makeshift 'Love Hut': a hideaway in the yard, handmade from scraps of wood with a palm-thatched roof and laundry hanging up to dry out the front.

There was no running water in the house so the toilet was flushed with buckets of water. We all ate together in the kitchen, which was mostly a joy except when Felix decided to splash out on something special one day. Looking mischievous, he pointed with his lips, as is the way in the Philippines, towards a bloody box on the floor. Inside was a gruesome-looking cow's head with its bloated tongue lolling out the side of its mouth. Despite my host's assurances to the contrary, that evening's soup was one of the worst things I've ever eaten.

The five women I worked with were shy and quiet, but we formed an easy bond, and soon got into a routine. Once they'd finished their morning chores I'd meet them and give them a hand with whatever they were making. I was amazed by how hard they worked, and by the creations they'd come up with despite possessing virtually no resources – my favourite were the colourful handbags made entirely of handmade beads. It felt as though I was learning a lot more from them than they were from me.

The warmth of the women, my host family and the rest of the village meant I quickly felt at home. Within the first week I'd tried the local delicacy, *balut*, a stomach-churning fertilised duck egg; cracked out a rendition of Oasis's 'Wonderwall' at a village videoke session; tasted (too much) Tanduay rum; and salsa danced to 2 Unlimited at a mountain fiesta. My biggest difficulty, apart from the 5 a.m. cockerel alarm clocks, wasn't any of the catastrophes I'd dreamt up before stepping on that boat. It was finding a minute to myself. Personal space is undesirable in the rural Philippines. Everyone lives in close proximity, some with up to fourteen siblings in one small hut. And life is precious, too often cut short, so they enjoy being together whether it's to sing corny K-pop songs or have dinner with a neighbour who's fallen on hard times.

I've since discovered there's often a moment of a trip, maybe just a few seconds, that sums up what that experience meant for you and stays with you long after all the initial insecurities and minor inconveniences have been forgotten.

For my first solo trip, in the Philippines, that moment is me on the back of a motorbike taxi, speeding round a bend on a dirt road with a lush, jungle-covered mountain on one side and the twinkling turquoise sea on the other. I had the wind in my hair (and up my skirt – I hadn't quite mastered the traveller's wardrobe), the warmth of the afternoon sun on my freckly face and an enormous grin I couldn't get rid of. There's a soundtrack for it too, when I think about that moment. It's a song I listened to a lot at the time by Perry Blake, with a beautiful melody that's always in motion and the most perfect title – 'This Life'. That moment for me was pure freedom, freedom like I'd never experienced it before, and it's this feeling, of life being lived, that still pushes me to do things I'm scared of. On my own.

Since the Philippines, **Hannah Stuart-Leach** has embarked on many one-woman wanders. Her favourites include a two-week beach holiday in Sri Lanka, which turned into an unforgettable five-month adventure, and a 400-mile solo hike through England, Scotland and Wales. She still gets nervous every time.

Tips

Remember that nerves can be a good thing. If you're nervous about the prospect of travelling alone it just means you're stretching yourself, doing something worth doing. *Hannah Stuart-Leach*

Try it. You can go home if you don't like it. *Janet Rogers*

Don't let the media colour your view of the world and its inhabitants. Ninety-nine per cent of people are wonderful and in my experience of travelling alone, even backpacking alone as a single female, I've always felt safe. On the ground with locals is a very different situation than viewing from the outside looking in. It's a cliché, but to push your travel boundaries means you buzz a little and appreciate 'normality' when you go back to it. *Claire Morsman*

Most solo travellers find dining alone can be embarrassing. I make it a conscious opportunity to enjoy good food, so eat at good restaurants, but as early as possible before the romantic couples arrive. I take a newspaper and do the crossword, or catch up with my diary, but never a book which seems too isolating. And once the meal comes I savour every mouthful, meet people's eyes and refuse to look shamefaced. It works. *Hilary Bradt*

Safety in Numbers

✛ ✛ ✛

Joining an organised group can be a logical step for people forced by circumstances to travel alone, and several of our writers took this route, often in unconventional ways, and learned from the experience. Ian Douglas felt at first like an oldie amongst chattering youngsters in northern Thailand on a trip he took to prove his mettle, yet he bonded with their guide and the backpackers too. Jane Vincent-Havelka found balm for her grief by walking with a small group in the Himalayas; this set her up for a lifetime of similar treks, while Hazel Pennington's cycle ride to Skye, part of a large and initially daunting crowd, was literally life-changing. In contrast, Phoebe Smith strikes gold in that riskiest of all solo risks – the shared cabin.

A Coconut with Three Candles
Ian Douglas

The Buddha seemed alive. A golden-skinned monk with his orange robe flapping in the balmy night. I sneaked off the cracked Bangkok pavements and into the deserted temple. Close up, he was just another beautiful statue.

But the temple wasn't deserted. The compound had its own security, Thai style – two flea-bitten street dogs lay dozing on the concrete. Maybe they were reincarnated guardians, for one sniff of my foreign scent and they immediately gave chase. Out of the temple and down the street, snapping at my heels. Ouch! One sank his fangs into my calf and drew blood. Satisfied, they trotted away.

Back at the youth hostel on Phitsanulok Road, the scruffy young backpackers were more worried than I was. I didn't want to be the silly old man, fussing about a scratch. The whole point of coming to Asia alone was to prove my mettle. I'd spent too long feeling sorry for myself after my girlfriend left and now it was time to start over. But the fresh-faced backpackers lectured me on the perils of rabies until I gave in. Midnight found me speeding in a tuk-tuk down empty streets, bound for the Mission Hospital.

I was expecting a dirty ward overcrowded with poor people. Instead, I found a pristine palace of medicine. And the treatment was painless enough. A simple injection in the shoulder and a card with dates for four follow-up shots I could get at any Thai hospital. But hardly a good start to my trip. A lot of nightmares that night.

The overnight train took me north. Wide-open windows blasted air through the carriage, cooling the tropical heat. I tucked into Singha beer and enjoyed the scenery. The darkness was alive with light. Sparks erupted from bonfires, lorries were draped with fairy lights, candles flickered inside tiny spirit houses. And overhead, never changing, the oldest lights of all. I raised a beer bottle and toasted Orion.

My destination was Chiang Mai. With a few days to kill between jabs, I looked into a hill tribe trek. The hill tribes migrated to southeast Asia a few hundred years ago. They recognise no national boundary and owe allegiance to no government. They must be anathema to Thai officialdom, but at least they draw in the tourists.

Chiang Mai's youth hostel boasted tours that did not parade the tribes around like circus performers. In fact, the hostel ran a programme of hill tribe assistance, in contrast to the myriad tour companies that milked the tourist market. So, naturally, I picked the youth hostel's offering.

A one-handed boy called Kobra announced he was to be our guide. His left arm ended in a clump of bandages. Ten guests identified themselves as being on the tour. They were a youthful bunch, Australians, Americans and Brits. I stared at them in silent horror. They were years younger than me. Would we bond or might the trek turn into four days of isolation? Me and a gang of twenty-somethings. What could we possibly have in common?

I had worse concerns. The thought of being up in the hills, miles from a hospital, gave me panic attacks. Supposing that blasted dog bite was infected and I got sick, without even an aspirin for relief?

A couple of ramshackle vans drove us for hours into the countryside. The hills grew steeper. Mango trees and frangipani gave way to rainforest. But it was very dry rainforest, dusty and ochre coloured. The drop-off point was a line of wooden shacks. Pigs were wallowing in mud, as were some children.

'This way,' Kobra said quietly, leading us over a fallen tree and up the grassy steps of the rice terraces. Below us the landscape fell away in opium fields and burnt land.

Social dynamics were forming. The backpackers were all chattering among themselves. They ignored me, the 'oldie'. They also ignored Kobra, as if he were the hired help. So I caught him up and tried a few words of conversation. At first he was reticent, serious, focused on his role as guide. But after a while he relaxed. I learned about his first job as a trainee car mechanic. One day he had stuck his hand into a car engine to fix something. His co-worker hadn't been aware of this and had switched on the ignition.

Losing a hand severely reduced his job chances. There's no welfare assistance in the developing world. He feared a life of begging until the youth hostel offered him this post. I could see how important it was to him. And he was still on probation. If he screwed things up he might face a sacking. Under my breath I vowed to be the ideal trekker, obedient and helpful.

Shortly before dusk we arrived at a Karen tribe village, a collection of huts on stilts, overlooking an untamed valley. Well, this was roughing it. No electricity, no plumbing, no furniture. Pigs, dogs and water buffalo lived under the stilted huts. A siphon, run from a well, served as our outdoor shower. Toilets were a question of the nearest bush. Many huts had seesaw-like contraptions outside them. A villager jumped on and off one end of the plank, causing the spiked, opposite end to pound a bowl of rice grains. Simple milling. Our porter arrived, carrying three days' worth of provisions on his shoulders.

'I cook you tea, first I finish opium,' he explained. Indeed, the men from the tribe never seemed to be without a fat cheroot in their mouths. Kobra sternly forbade us from cadging a joint. He warned us that bush opium was strong stuff and said a backpacker had died after sampling some. Nobody had any inclination to flout his advice.

Dusk was falling fast, swallowing up the palm trees. Somebody, somewhere, had a radio. The mournful chords of Black's 'Wonderful Life' filled the air. Never had a random pop song seemed so apt.

After rice and vegetables, the children sang us 'Frère Jacques'. Then a spider the size of a rat appeared in our midst. Cue ten Westerners screaming like babies. Kobra came in and stomped the poor creature. In retrospect, I suspect one of the kids had shoved the unfortunate arachnid through the floorboards for a lark. Ten of us bedded down on the bare, splintery wood. I had the deepest, most tranquil sleep of my life.

Waking next day to the reek of burning logs, we scurried to and from the well, weighed down by an array of insect repellents, sunblocks, deodorants, soaps and shampoos. The village children were completely baffled by our clutter.

After breakfast, our ride turned up – elephants! Elephant back is *the* way to travel. And those kindly beasts would, from time to time, suck up a puddle and spray the water over their heads. It was most refreshing in the heat of the day. The endless chatter of my co-trekkers was proving tiresome, though. I stole away to the river and watched children splashing and laughing. Water shimmered in the sunlight as I contemplated my journey. They had so little, yet seemed so happy. I was wealthy by comparison, yet weighed down with worries – about my failed relationship, my lack of connection with the other trekkers. Was it them, or was it me who was standoffish? I still had no answers.

The next leg of the journey was uphill and we looked like soaked beetroots when we reached the summit. A village of the Lawa people nestled in the valley below. It was a mosaic of tin roofs, glinting like rubies in the sunset. This village boasted an icebox. Oh such treasure – lollies, sodas, fizzy pop and even drinking water. I gulped down the liquid like a man lost in a desert. Is there any greater pleasure in life than quenching a thirst?

One of my fellow trekkers was Beatrice, a London nurse. It just so happened to be her birthday. After the rice and vegetable dinner, Kobra magically conjured up a coconut with three candles poking out. In our state of cheerful exhaustion this seemed the funniest jape ever. Suddenly, we were all laughing like old friends and singing 'Happy Birthday'. The age gap evaporated. Maybe it had never existed. Had I imagined the whole thing? Who knows, but now we were equals, friends and trekkers.

Later, I strolled away, stargazing, with a dazzling view of the Milky Way. Kobra came and found me. I marvelled at how industrious this boy was – up before us every morning, scrambling eggs and boiling rice, then leading us through the jungle all day, displaying endless patience for our foibles and tantrums, motivating us up that steep incline, massaging our aching bodies, solving every worry.

'If the trekkers are happy, I am happy,' he said.

I realised he was shattered. But he could not knock off until every guest was tucked up for the night. Including me. Hardly able to stand, he led me back to the hut and sent me to bed.

An ear-splitting cockerel's call woke me in time to see the dawn. The sun peeked over the eastern ridge, rays bouncing across the valley and off the tin roofs. The morning light transformed the red of the soil to a pure purple. Fluffy specks of cumulus decorated the rich blue sky. Trees cast long shadows across the land, underlining the rugged contours.

The highlight of the third day was a waterfall, deep in the rainforest, where we showered after hours of sweaty saturation. We stopped at another village that night. I crept out of our shack for a pee around midnight. Crickets chirruped. Frogs croaked. Stars glittered. A pinpoint of blue light fluttered out of the blackness – my first firefly.

Day four reunited us with civilization. We were glad to see things like mattresses and refrigerators, yet sad to say goodbye to the hilltops and the life there, free of modern-day angst. And then it occurred to me that during the trip I'd completely forgotten about my dog bite and my fears of getting sick in the boondocks. My anxieties all felt rather silly now.

Everyone was keen to take Kobra for dinner as a way of thanking him. As we gathered around the large table, Kobra said, 'I must sit next to Ian, for he is my brother.' I was touched.

Green curry and Mekong whisky flowed. Meanwhile, amidst all the jolly banter, Kobra quietly confided to me that he had recently lost both his parents. The last piece clicked in. It explained why he came across as so serious and determined. I wished him success with the rest of his life. For four days Kobra had guided me on a journey that would provide memories for a lifetime.

There were lessons as well as memories. Aftershave and electricity are not essential for existence. There's only an age gap if you allow there to be one. And everyone has a reason why they are the way they are. But anyone can change. Even me.

London-born **Ian Douglas** wanted to write from an early age. His family and teachers said this was a foolish notion and insisted he abandon the idea. Perhaps this is why he never settled in his first career as a social  worker. Aged thirty-one he gave it up to backpack around the world. He enjoyed east Asia so much he stayed for a decade teaching English. Today he lives with his family in Nottingham, working as a freelance writer and travelling whenever possible. Recent trips include South Africa, Florida and Berlin. His website is at www.iandouglas-writer.com.

The Start of a Passion

Jane Vincent-Havelka

'You need to start living again. Think of a new passion. Where would you like to travel?'

'To see the Himalayas again.'

'Then *go* for it!'

A friend's challenge was the start of a new direction in life. My husband, George, had died five years earlier, suddenly and unexpectedly. South America had been our focus for seventeen years, travelling in remote areas, writing and teaching. Now I was frozen, unable to make decisions. I had to move on.

A year later, in October, I found myself flying to Kathmandu, Nepal, for a three-week trek in the Annapurna area. This would also be a celebration of my fiftieth birthday. But my heart sank when I saw my companions – three British men, all tall, athletic and confident. I was a keen hiker, but this was daunting. Our guide was a quiet, older Nepalese man, Nawang, a former Buddhist monk who had been on an Everest expedition.

At the first chance I took him aside. 'I don't think I will be able to keep up with the men,' I said.

He patted me on the arm, and said quietly, 'Don't worry. I will help you. Often the fastest trekkers run into trouble first.'

To my surprise, right from day one we formed a close-knit group. The others were also travelling solo while searching for new meaning in their lives, and we were soon sharing our histories and hopes. Ian and Tim were in their forties. Dave was younger and faster, and Nawang was right: he was the one who suffered knee problems. We started some traditions, including a game of bridge as soon as we reached camp, and Ian had brought along a bottle of Baileys for a sip last thing at night before we headed to our tents.

Our trek started from Pokhara with the glorious peak of Machapuchare, 'Fish Tail Mountain', facing us. We had good weather, clear skies and hot days, although the nights were freezing. The scenery was out of this world. We passed through stone villages of various ethnic groups, often accessed by hundreds of rough stone steps, and negotiated trails that wound up and down mountainsides against a backdrop of snowy peaks. We continued past the massif of the Annapurnas. Dhaulagiri, at 8,167 metres the seventh-highest mountain in the world, became our ever-present inspiration. I felt such a sense of spirituality; but also intense sorrow, as I thought of my loss. At such times, Nawang sensed my sadness and we had long discussions about life and death during which he tried to give me hope for the future.

The enormous canyon of the Kali Gandaki River lay far below. Mountains stretched in all directions. We marvelled at the sunrises and sunsets. There were many times when I couldn't believe I was really there. I thought of what had been my husband's motto in life: 'The things we regret are the things we didn't have the courage to do.' I had found the courage to travel alone, and this was my reward.

Early each morning we heard Nawang chanting and spinning his prayer wheel in his tent. He often did this while walking the trail.

He showed us how much of what we saw was part of a Buddhist's daily life. Dozens of *chortens*, small stone mounds and monuments, were built over sacred scriptures and relics. Long rows of prayer wheels lined the trails in the countryside and villages, and we encountered people in colourful dress walking along, spinning their individual prayer wheels. We came across walls, and piles of *mani* stones carved with sacred inscriptions. Thousands of prayer flags hung from poles and trees. Monasteries were painted with a reddish-brown stripe at the top. Anything sacred had to be passed in a clockwise direction to show respect.

The trek threw everything at me. I was an experienced hiker and thankful I was in good shape. Yes, the men were faster, but they were always considerate and never competitive. I had a fear of bridges, yet our route was dotted with high and shaky bridges over canyons and roaring rivers, and very long suspension bridges that swung over wider rivers. Fortunately, Dave hated them as much as I did and so we'd cross them in single file with Ian and Tim going first and last. In this way they could prevent any of the locals from dashing across with their animals or making the bridges swing vigorously on purpose. Whenever we came to stepping stones over rushing streams, Nawang provided a steady hand.

I hated scree slopes, and there were plenty where landslides had occurred. Nawang led the way and we all provided warnings and practical suggestions, and moral support to each other. Our porters, while carrying the most unbelievable loads, would stop to crack a joke or lend a hand.

Female friends had urged me to wear a skirt. On the first day I saw the reason. Often there were no bushes or rocks around when nature called, and I learned to squat gracefully, like the local women, with my full skirt providing some privacy.

At that time, there were no lodges along the route. Our camp crew usually beat us to the campsite and had our tents up and tea waiting. Often we pitched our tents wherever Nawang had friends. Once it was on the roof of a sturdy house, with the pegs driven into the hardened mud and a notched wooden ladder leading down to the outhouse. Another time it was in a courtyard and we were invited to sit around the owners' fire. We appreciated the hospitality, but the acrid smoke was hard to take. At other times, we pitched camp in a field with the donkeys or on a mountainside. We met very few other tourists.

We had been provided with sturdy wooden poles with a pointed fork at the top. We were very conscious of safety since there was no medical help for injuries. The rule was to walk or look, but not both. Then, far up the trail, I stopped to look at the scenery, my foot stepped on a loose rock, and the point of my hiking pole went into my right eye. I remember feeling very calm and thinking: *Even if I lose my sight, this trek will have been worth it.* We put a large pad on the eye, with lots of strapping to keep it immobile, but by evening the side of my face was swollen and bruised.

It made an interesting subject of conversation in all the villages. What I didn't realise was that I had lost my depth perception and for the rest of the trek I would have to 'feel' every footstep. It was nerve wracking in mountainous terrain. It wasn't until almost the end of the walk that we met a German trekking party with a doctor. He was able to tell me that, by a stroke of luck, the tip had missed the centre of the eye and I would regain my sight.

Further on, the scenery and weather became wilder. We were crossing treeless plateaus with chains of mountains in the distance. We trekked for hours up a dry river, with the fierce wind stirring up clouds of sand, and pitched our tents behind the stone walls of a village house to protect them from being blown away. Reaching the large village of Kagbeni in Upper Mustang, a young monk wanted to show us his monastery with its rows of prayer wheels. Finally, we arrived at the sacred pilgrimage site of Muktinath. Here, a Hindu priest, sensing my grief, sat with me and passed on his wisdom for over an hour. How interesting that the healing on this trek came from a Buddhist, a Hindu – and my three new companions.

Our furthest point was Thorung La, a pass at 5,416 metres; here we turned round. Our trek did not include the whole Annapurna circuit, which would have needed more time than we could spare. Instead, we returned to Pokhara, but on a different route in an attempt to make it slightly easier for me with my limited eyesight. My companions were quite happy to negotiate parts of the trail by steep steps to avoid landslides.

What an amazing trip it had been. And how lucky I had been with my guide and companions. My confidence was back. I could move on with my life. I still missed my partner deeply, but I could see a new way forward, a way that included the travel I had come to love during our marriage.

For more than twenty-five years since then I have explored Asia, and have returned to trek in the Himalayan mountains eleven more times. I look for active trips, usually involving trekking, and often for as long as a month. Most times I have signed on with a small group, since a guide and equipment are necessary for trekking. I have learned to take mountain challenges – goat-ledge trails, bridges, steep slopes, high passes and glaciers – calmly and in all types of weather. Occasionally I've travelled with a close friend or my daughter. But I've discovered I love travelling solo in India,

Cambodia, China, Nepal, Burma and Indonesia. Time is my own. I can choose where to go and what to see and how long to spend. I have met other travellers sharing the same approach to life, made new international friends, received help and hospitality from local people and, as a photographer, enjoyed the chance to take thousands of unique photos.

My life is interesting, fun and rich, in large part thanks to all the opportunities gained by having the courage to travel solo. And thanks to my friend who urged me to '*Go* for it!'

Jane Vincent-Havelka is a Canadian photographer and writer living in London, Ontario. For over twenty-five years Jane has concentrated on Asia for her work, with a particular  interest in how the people and their cultures are affected by economic, political and environmental issues.

The Social Mobility of Cycling

Hazel Pennington

*O*K, I told myself as the clubhouse loomed, *get in there and join in*. I walked boldly through the door to see a mass of strangers packed around maybe twenty tables – everyone, so it seemed, talking animatedly. The noise was impressive. There wasn't a soul I recognised. No-one was looking out for me. In a matter of half a second I had made a radical revision to my plan for the evening. An hour or so of lying on a wafer of foam in my minuscule tent reading by torchlight was, I now saw, how I really wanted to spend the evening.

For someone used to travelling with a partner, it had already been a big decision to throw in my lot with 160 strangers, cycling from London to the Isle of Skye. Indeed, I had agonised for weeks before finally, on the now-or-never principle, booking only days before the start. With some effort – physical and psychological – I had managed to get myself to the first campsite. But the uproarious clubhouse was, for the first evening at any rate, a step too far. Things did not augur well, socially speaking, for the next fortnight.

There was always Plan B. I had a good friend in York I'd already sounded out, just in case. If I could last that far – just three more days – I could bale out and stay with her for a day or two before heading home, tail well and truly between my legs, to face the questions of my friends. But would I be able to survive the ignominy of three whole days of being Norma-no-Mates?

As group holidays go, this one was, as I now know, challenging. With the majority of group tours there are maybe ten to twenty-five people, so you normally walk or cycle together and by the end of the first day you've spoken to everyone. We were of course far too many for that. We had route notes and maps and were free to set off in our own time and cycle as quickly or as slowly as we pleased. Given my sedate pace the tendency was for people to appear alongside me, chat for a bit, then after a few minutes shoot off ahead. So for the next couple of days I was essentially alone and at sea in this boisterous crowd.

The meals at the campsites – breakfast, afternoon tea and supper – were easy enough. We would queue for a plate of food and then sit down wherever there was a space at one of the big trestle tables laid out in the marquee. Here it was natural to engage your neighbours in conversation. But at coffee or lunchtime I would pass pubs and cafés almost hidden behind the massed bikes and be quite unable to pluck up the courage to go in. I was reluctant to impose myself on an already-established group.

As the miles went by I started to see that there were others who had come alone and, like me, were not necessarily the life and soul of the party. I got a little braver. By York, though I still hadn't exactly found my feet, I knew I was going to continue. I could by now recognise quite a few faces in the teeming masses and, besides, I had become fascinated by the way not simply the scenery, but also the architecture and the accents, changed between breakfast and supper. There was a real sense that we were on a journey.

I was also discovering that as I pedalled along beside someone, perhaps for miles, conversation could lurch remarkably quickly from bland generalities to whatever was at that point central to the person's life. The stages of developing friendship were getting concentrated into an unusually short space of time. Perhaps doing something that is often exhausting, in the midst of strangers, exposes your vulnerabilities, so that the social niceties become less relevant and you get straight to the centre of things. One particular aspect of cycling in a group – what someone referred to later as the 'social mobility of cycling' – played its part in mixing us all up. Any interruption to the flow of pedalling – a junction, a bit of street theatre, a café stop, a steep hill – would change the line-up, and so several times a day you would find yourself beside someone different. Some promising conversations never did get finished, but new ones took their place.

Almost imperceptibly, the stimulation of getting to know so many new people began to bewitch me. It was akin to student life concentrated into a single two-week burst of energy and exhaustion, high spirits and disappointments, discovery, challenging discussions, late nights, in-jokes, evanescent groups, gossip, hard work and lasting friendships.

As the days unfolded and those all-important links were made, the preoccupations of life back home became less clamorous, to the point where home began to feel like something in a different, distant existence. Life on this tour was simple. Our basic needs were met. Tents and luggage were delivered every day to the next campsite. Breakfast, afternoon tea and supper were provided. Company – lots of it – was on hand. And each day we had a clearly defined purpose – to get ourselves and our bikes to the day's destination. This became the overriding concern, and the persistent cold headwind and uniformly grey skies that made this task more challenging only served to bond us more.

By Richmond we were beginning to feel like a village on the move. We had by now been through a lot together and the acceptance and forbearance generally displayed by family and neighbours to other members of the clan were emerging. We knew the larger-than-life characters who stood out from the crowd, the ones who wanted only to discuss sprockets, the people you could rely on for a sympathetic hearing. It was of course impossible to know everyone, but the group and the whole set-up felt familiar, and we were at ease sharing tales of derring-do (or at least of the ongoing battle with the headwind, or how we ran out of chocolate) over supper with people we'd never met before. There were now lots of acquaintances to greet and pass the time of day with and to catch up on the latest gossip. This largely involved speculation on budding romances – but also occasionally on cracks showing in friendships or relationships – the bush telegraph being remarkably efficient, and possibly a tad creative, on these occasions.

At some point in each day – usually when the combination of headwind and long miles was making itself felt in tired muscles – we were helped on our way by the antics of the splendid Bath-based Natural Theatre Company, members of which accompanied us the whole way. We rapidly learned to expect surreal goings-on. One day we had cleaners at dawn, arriving in our midst at 6.30 a.m. bedecked in headscarves and overalls, keen to eject us from our tents so that they could get on with the hoovering. I remember being inordinately pleased when, toiling up a steep lane, I saw an immaculately dressed waiter rise up on the other side of the hedge to pass me a glass of sherry on a silver tray. It was a brilliant way of breaking up the journey. And when we reached the Scottish border we were greeted by a wildly long-haired, ginger-bearded and kilted Highlander with a suspiciously impenetrable accent, who demanded our passports before sitting us down on a roadside chair to drink a nip of his finest whisky and to pose with him for a souvenir photograph.

In Scotland the sun finally appeared and we basked in the sudden warmth. As we got closer to the west coast a party atmosphere was developing, a sort of suppressed almost-end-of-term excitement. On the long and winding road to Mallaig, the nurse and mechanic who patrolled the route each day to deal with any emergencies kept checking up on us like mother ducks to ensure we would all make it in time for the ferry to Skye. In the event we all did, and the atmosphere was tremendous. To the sound of bagpipes we had a final short ride to the Clan Donald Centre where our arrival prompted the popping of many champagne corks. At the party that night, we discovered the huge amount of talent there was in the group as cyclists sang, played instruments that had undertaken the journey in the luggage lorry, deejayed and generally larked about till the early hours.

Inevitably there were tears the next morning as people packed up to catch the special train south. I didn't leave with them. With new-found friends I was staying on Skye for a couple of days before continuing north to Harris, where we stayed in a traditional croft and explored wild landscapes and beautiful beaches in the clover-scented air.

This, my first experience of going away with strangers, was life changing in the most positive way. At its simplest, I had seen some beautiful parts of England and Scotland and found I could have a brilliant holiday without the support of partner, family or friends. I also discovered that there are lots of people out there with whom one can easily, and rewardingly, connect; that however unpromising a first contact with someone might be, everyone has a story to tell; and that once the ice is broken with a new group, there are lots of laughs to be had.

And my life really was transformed. After the tour I felt restless and finally decided to take the risk of giving up my safe, secure teaching job. About three years and several holidays with different companies later, I eventually found myself moving to Bath and working for the organisers of the London to Skye ride. One of my many tasks was to cycle on any new tours, wherever in the world that might be, to ensure all the complicated logistics worked smoothly. While I had been working out my notice, still unclear about how I was going to keep body and soul together, I had sometimes joked with friends that I was looking for someone to pay me to go cycling. To my everlasting astonishment and gratitude, I had done precisely that.

Hazel Pennington has worked in IT, taught languages and helped organise bicycle tours. She has cycled on four continents – most often in Europe – and stays in touch with fellow travellers in various parts of the world. She is fascinated by the processes by which a group of strangers so quickly becomes a group of trusted friends.

Not so Solo at Sea
Phoebe Smith

I'd never felt this afraid to open a door. While standing on this side of it, in the comfort of ignorance, anything could be waiting for me. But once I'd opened it, once I'd taken the plunge and was faced with whatever or, more accurately, whomever lay beyond, there was no going back.

I took a deep breath, squeezed the handle and pushed the door open.

Going solo has never put me off travel. It's not that I'm antisocial; it's just that sometimes the idea of heading off into a wild place with everything I need in my backpack to be self-sufficient, with no-one to rely on or fight with over a map, is a true escape.

But the problem with going solo on organised trips – for those of us like me who genuinely love solitude – is that very often you don't actually get to be alone at all. In fact, you're usually seen less as a single entity and more of a handy odd number that can fill in the inconvenient gaps, such as a middle seat in a plane row or the spare chair between couples on a lunch table. No, if you're going alone and you really want to get some time alone, you usually have to pay for the privilege in the form of a single supplement. This is usually worth the extra cash, until it comes to one type of trip – an expedition cruise.

I should point out this is no 'Cruise' with a capital C. Forget luxury bedrooms, cheesy entertainment and set tables for mealtimes. Expedition cruises are all about the adventure of going to far-flung places only accessible by sea. Think the Arctic, the Galápagos or Antarctica. The ships are usually repurposed icebreakers or industrial vessels that have been made comfortable but serve a purpose – to voyage into the extremes. As such, the people who go on them are usually well-travelled and audacious and, very often, solo travellers. However, on this type of journey each traveller pays for the bed, not the room. You can pay twice to guarantee your own space, but for most this is prohibitively expensive.

I shrugged it off, unconcerned, when I first booked my trip to Antarctica. But the closer my departure date came, the more the reality set in – I was going to have to share my cabin, my personal space, with a complete stranger for no less than three weeks. It was quite honestly the scariest prospect of my life. This was going solo without the benefits of being alone.

I packed earplugs – in case they were a snorer; an eye mask – in case they wanted to sleep with the light on; a good book – to hide behind and avoid the dreaded small talk; an iPad and headphones preloaded with all my favourite shows – in case the book didn't work and... chocolate – to use as a peace offering if needed.

So, when I stepped up to the cabin door on the ship, half excited to be heading to the White Continent, half terrified to be discovering whom fate had paired me up with, I was as prepared as I could be.

As it happened, behind my creaky wooden door was a similarly aged woman whom for anonymity's sake I'll call Susie. Originally from Shanghai but having worked for the last ten years in New York, she had managed to bag this trip last minute on the cheap while hanging out in the port town of Ushuaia on a six-month career break. I smiled as she told me this, thinking how I might have had the room all to myself if it wasn't for the company putting on such a bargain last-minute price.

'I've just had a nightmare in the hostel – people were so noisy,' she confessed, studying my face for a reaction. And then it dawned on me – we were each clearly as nervous as the other. I was as much an unknown entity to her as she was to me.

We established some ground rules very quickly. She told me she'd already chosen her bed and cupboard, but then offered me the extra bedside drawer to make up for it. For the next hour we unpacked, being super polite, incredibly cautious, careful not to offend. When the first meal was called we went together and sat at the same table, still trying to work one another out. That night we gave each other a respectful amount of time in the cupboard-sized bathroom, said goodnight and agreed to turn out the light. As I lay there trying to get to sleep, listening to the strange sound of another person lightly snoring just a couple of feet away from me, I wondered how long our very polite relationship could possibly continue.

In the morning we had our first day at sea on the notorious Drake Passage, a stretch of water renowned to test the sea legs of even the saltiest of sea dogs. During the mandatory safety lecture I sat with some other solo travellers who started to share the gossip on their cabin mates. Everyone had been petrified to meet each other and though most were getting on well, two were already not speaking due to a bad night's sleep. I laughed as someone described trying to explain good cabin etiquette to her non-English-speaking cabin mate who'd insisted on eating a very pungent-smelling food at 3 a.m., feeling quite smug that all I'd had to endure was some gentle snoring.

Then I started to feel that something was very wrong. I began to feel hot and shivery. I knew instantly what it was – seasickness.

Despite administering a patch before I left port, I felt impossibly grim. As the lecture ended I started down the stairs feeling queasy, struggling to walk straight as the ship lurched from side to side. As soon as I caught sight of our cabin door, without any hesitation I ran for it and immediately threw up in the toilet.

I thought Susie would be horrified. I know I was, but she appeared as if from nowhere and began to help. From holding my hair back to getting me on to the bed, then fetching the doctor, it was like having a nurse on call. She brought me a cola to help my stomach, went to pick up my Muck boots for the rest of the trip, and then left me to sleep. Later she came back to check up on me, making sure I didn't want for anything. I felt utterly blessed. My annoyance at having to share a cabin was now replaced with thanks.

The next few days, as I found my sea legs, we developed the perfect cabin relationship and it turned out our sleeping habits complemented each other perfectly. While I liked to get up early to head out on deck she would sleep in and only surface as breakfast finished, meaning no queue for the shower. In the evening she liked to stay out longer with her friends, meaning I'd often be asleep before she was back and started snoring. But it was our approach to the actual sightseeing that I found most amusing.

While Susie seemingly aimed to be the last one off the ship in an effort to keep warm as long as possible, I always took advantage of my solo status to fill any gaps on earlier Zodiacs, desperate to be among the first to walk among the king penguins and watch the icebergs calve. While I was running around in Grytviken trying to soak up all the historical sites where Shackleton famously set forth on his ill-fated *Endurance* expedition and was later buried, she was far more excited about having her photo taken with some troops from the British Army stationed there. When we returned to our cabin and shared our experiences, it sounded as though we'd each been on a completely different stop. It had me in fits of laughter.

Not everyone on the ship was as lucky as I was, of course. A group of three got so annoyed with each other that one of them asked to move rooms, while another pairing had a blazing row on the second night about which side of the room they wanted to be on – though even they, in the end, realised that it was more about what lay outside the room than what was in it, and that a little bit of tolerance went a long way.

Some pairings became firm friends, promising to accompany one another on a similar cruise again. With Susie and me, she found her group, I found mine. But as such we always had plenty to talk about back in the cabin; and though we made no plans to journey with each other again, we both looked forward to our chats each evening.

'I think we were very lucky,' she said to me on the final day as we sat on our beds and looked through the drawers, all cabin boundaries gone out the porthole as we struggled to repack our respective suitcases. 'We were both nice,' she added.

I nodded.

Back at port it was finally time for my treat – one final night in Ushuaia in a hotel room on my own. The sheer luxury of it made me giddy with excitement. I spent the day out sightseeing, walking in Tierra del Fuego National Park and chatting to locals in a bar. Finally I headed back for bed and then it hit me.

There would be no-one putting on the television while I was trying to read a book, no gentle snoring as I turned out the light.

But by the same token there would be no-one to share my stories with, no-one to proudly boast to about how I'd managed to tick off all the major museums in town and still found time to try the killer empanadas in the local bakery, and no-one to laugh about the day with. For someone who loves solitude I'd come to realise that sometimes, just sometimes, sharing a room with a stranger can help you enjoy the trip even more. I smiled and, just for a second, waited on this side of the door a little longer.

Award-winning travel editor, writer, speaker, presenter and author **Phoebe Smith** has seen her love of wild places take her on solo adventures all around the world – from wild camping on the Scottish islands to portaledging in trees in the Bavarian Alps and bedding down inside glaciers in Svalbard,  the last stop before the North Pole. She is the editor of *Wanderlust*, the UK's best adventure travel magazine, and is author of seven books including *Extreme Sleeps: Adventures of a Wild Camper*, *The Book of the Bothy*, and the inspiring *Wilderness Weekends: Wild Adventures in Britain's Rugged Corners*, published by Bradt Travel Guides and showcasing some of the country's most isolated spots – places perfect for a solo trip.

Tips

If travelling solo in a group…

Often an activity, such as cycling or art galleries, can create a common interest.

Decide if you would prefer to be with your own age group. Is a mix of ages better for you?

If you're a bit shy, have a few snippets of small talk ready: discussing previous holidays, food or your expectations of the journey are easy, relaxed opening topics.

A tour guide should be used to getting a group to gel. They have loads of information, and may well be able to introduce you to others.

Some companies run forums so it's possible to meet fellow travellers before departure. It's a good way to learn about solo travel, even if you just read the posts and comments. On your return, visit the forum again as positive comments may encourage others to take the plunge.

On safety when travelling alone...

Should you get lost, do ask for directions but say you are meeting a friend if you'd prefer not to advertise that you're on your own. Clutching a guidebook can be a bit obvious too, so read up information before you set off.

When dealing with unwelcome advances – well, my granny recommended a hatpin, which is not the best idea! The problem with walking away briskly is that you can be followed. 'My partner/son/daughter is joining me in a moment' can work; dashing into the nearest loo has some success, or, in desperation, say loudly, 'Go away please, now!' This way, you also alert those nearby to your situation.

From *Silver Travel Advisor* (travel reviews and advice for the over 50s) www.silvertraveladvisor.com

A single supplement may be expensive, but be cautious about sharing a room with a stranger. Although as a tour leader I've seen life-long friendships forged this way, I remember trips spoiled by incompatible roommates; my heart sank on behalf of one woman when I heard her new roommate explain: 'I always carry a piece of chalk to mark out my half of the room.' Bear in mind, also, that most older people snore. You may be able to book a cruise cabin with no single supplement if you book early, are flexible with your dates and destination, and perhaps use the help of a cruise agent. *Hilary Bradt*

Travel with a Purpose

✥ ✥ ✥

Many reluctant solos choose volunteering as their entry into travelling alone. Apart from the pleasure of doing some good in the world, the framework of somewhere to stay and a daily programme is reassuring. Vicki Brown discovers her childhood dream of rainforest in the remote jungle of Ecuador and, surprisingly, 'in Wimbí I ached to be lonely' (Hannah Stuart-Leach, facing her fear in the Philippines, has the same problem). Other writers find purpose in rural France, or pet-sitting to explore some wilder parts of New South Wales. Elspeth Cardy seeks a task to combat the feeling that travelling alone is selfish, as does Christine Green, although she needs a break from the exhaustion of the lambing shed on her sheep farm. When her misgivings persist, she reminds herself 'this wasn't something I *had* to do' and that her family have encouraged her to take this pick-me-up, which becomes part of her farming year.

Getting Going Again
Elspeth Cardy

I sometimes go to sleep dreaming of this journey. The tiny hamlet by the coast is reached by a single-track road that winds over olive-clad hills and down the other side to the sea. The land here is privately owned and occupied by vineyards, so there is no development and no buildings apart from the chateaux. It's just vineyards, then tall pine trees leaning gracefully over soft sand beaches. The coast here is laced with coves, fringed by a coastal path and lapped by clear waters. The hamlet is simply a few houses, with no shop or bar; there's a small hotel and a man in a hut near the path to the beach, selling bread in the morning, and a 'dish of the day' to take away in the evening. It is years since I've been there.

In May, I turn the mattress and open wide the windows. A kind of nostalgia sweeps over me, a longing that is strong – to go forth and meet the spring, to travel south and plunge into that cool turquoise sea. I think this is partly a yearning for travel, but also a yearning for past times. I remember how my father used to stand in pale Scottish sunshine, leaning on his fork, a drip forming at the end of his nose over the neat rows of sprouts, carrots, leeks, raspberries and strawberries. And then we'd travel, packed into a car adapted for sleeping children as we drove through the night. I also recall a work visit to Rome in early spring; and the bright colours of Rwanda and travelling alone.

So what stops me now? What is this strange reluctance? I have the time, and I can afford to go. But after years of work taking up every spare bit of energy, with my identity shaped by meaningful work, and living with a partner who still works full on, how do I leave? How to justify such a selfish act? And what should I do, now that lying for days on end on a beach has lost its appeal?

If I go away with my partner, it's a holiday for much-needed rest, walks and cultural visits. But travel, for me, is a solo venture – a time to test one's resources and enjoy another culture, a time for hearing and speaking another language. There's a little nagging voice telling me I can't do this anymore, that I'll be lonely and at a loss, and that I'll only fret about how everyone is doing at home. This voice has to be silenced and another voice summoned, one reminding me that I love travel, that I am good at it and I can go off on my own because I used to do it a lot, and to places much more far-flung than just across the Channel.

I need a project, something to give me a reason for a trip. But still, the idea feels just a little alarming.

And then, a project drops into my lap. It's a bit of a fluke, but a small and reputable travel company advertises new holidays in an area near to those favourite places I have neglected for years. They have nothing for one or two people; it's all big villas for house parties. Cheekily, I ask if they have anything smaller, and if not, whether they would like help finding suitable places. It comes as something of a shock next day when they reply, saying, 'Yes, please.' It's a sign, so I must do it.

Within a few days arrangements are made. Having suggested a dozen or so small hotels and self-catering properties that might suit them, I have agreed to go and do a recce, take photos and write a report. I am leaving the following week, and I now have the perfect excuse to head off. I have 'a job', albeit unpaid.

It's a while since I've got on a plane, preferring the train if at all possible these days. It's even longer since I've headed off on my own. But of course it's not really hard and it's not very far. I step out of the plane on to a sun-beaten tarmac, greeting the hot dry brightness of more southerly climes. I've always enjoyed driving abroad, and here I am again, on my favourite drive over those blue olive-clad hills and down the other side to the vineyards and the pine-fringed beaches. It feels joyful. I am exhilarated to be here on my own, and with an excuse to try out that little hotel beside the beach.

I spend a few days visiting hotels and self-catering houses. I travel to medieval hill villages, with cobbled streets and flower-filled alleys, and views that draw the eye down to the islands off the coast. I visit small seaside towns and villages, where markets, colours and smells tempt the senses. It feels good to be back.

Back home again, I doubt whether I've found anything to meet the exacting standards of the travel company. But I have certainly found a host of places with character, simplicity and charm that I for one would be more than happy to perch in for days on end. I've been met with nothing but friendliness, and have had lots of opportunities to brush up my slightly rusty French.

The trip revives me. I've felt useful. I've had a purpose. It has topped up my confidence in myself and strengthened my belief in others to do without me for a while. I am left pondering on the wisdom of encouraging a company to enter this lovely world and fill it with tourists. But I am also wondering how to help the many single solo women travellers such as Sally, whom I met on her own in a small hotel by the sea. Recently divorced, she wanted somewhere she could visit and feel OK being on her own in, a place where she wouldn't be surrounded by loving couples, or happy family groups, and where people would be kind to her. That surely is something worth doing.

After a career in national and international education, **Elspeth Cardy** now works freelance as an executive coach and enjoys seeing the changes people make in their lives and careers. She also loves travelling; nothing energises her more than trundling off somewhere, pulling a small case or carrying a rucksack, hopefully having remembered her sketch book.

Where Everyone Knows Your Name
Vicki Brown

'Myyy naaame eeees… Bicki! Myyy naaame eeees… Bicki!' It was 6.30 a.m., and I had been abruptly awoken by a chorus of children marching past my hut, all of them apparently called 'Bicki'.

I tugged the edge of my mosquito net out from under my mattress and stepped on to the rough wooden floor. The equatorial sun was already burning; village life had begun. I pulled on my bikini, picked up my towel and stumbled sleepily down the slippery stones to the river behind my hut that doubled as my bathtub.

'Gudge mor-ning!' my neighbour Cecilia called brightly, as she marched confidently over the stones with a huge plastic tub full of clothes balanced on her head, ready to be washed in the river. It was Saturday, laundry day – and my day off teaching English to the women and children of Wimbí, in the remote tropical province of Esmeraldas, Ecuador.

I had dreamed of visiting the rainforest since I was a little girl growing up in the English countryside. Like all the children in my village, I lived life in the woods – climbing trees, spotting squirrels and foxes, delighting in the carpets of bluebells each spring and crunchy leaves each autumn. The woods were my favourite place, and in my head the rainforest was a supersized version with taller trees, vaster

124

leaves, bigger, noisier wildlife and thousands and thousands of miles of undisturbed nature to disappear into. Thinking about it made my stomach flip. But I was nine years old, I'd never left England, and I simply had no idea how one went about going to the jungle.

Seventeen years, one transatlantic flight, a six-hour bus ride, an overnight stopover and an eight-hour odyssey of trucks, minibuses and dugout canoes later – and I knew *exactly* how one went about getting to the jungle.

This was my journey to the tiny village of Wimbí, where I would be volunteering as an English teacher for one month as part of a project to encourage tourism to the area. The trip was a dream, but it was also the furthest I had ever been from home and friends and I was alone. Not only that – I was close to nine thousand miles from the nearest person I knew. And it would be weeks before I saw a familiar face again. Being alone was one thing; being this distant – in a place with no internet and no phone coverage – was more than I could comprehend at that moment. Exhausted, excited and very nervous, I made small talk with the other passengers and flicked through the guidebook, which stopped far short of where I was heading, in an effort to distract myself from the panic that bubbled just beneath the surface. I was a stranger to everyone.

Dusk was falling as I wrenched my sweaty body out of the cramped minibus filled with provisions for the village: rice, sugar, flour, chickens, vegetables, Pilsner and large bottles of Frontera – the local, lethal cane rum. As I stepped out, I saw the jungle with my own eyes for the first time, and it was more beautiful than I'd even imagined. While the last of the light lingered, I stood and contemplated what lay across the river – a thirty-metre wall of vegetation, a giant green speaker blasting the sounds of strange birds and shrieking cicadas. This was an IMAX projection of my childhood fantasy, and throughout the month I spent in Wimbí, I never quite managed to get over it.

It didn't take me long to adjust to village life, though. I was assigned a caring but strict 'jungle mum', Agueda, who cooked my meals, washed my clothes in the river and chased away the young men who tried to talk to me. As I washed in the river each morning, the men of the village poled past in dugout canoes, heading deeper into the rainforest to fell trees and haul them down to waiting chainsaws. Then I was left alone with the women – the only foreigner, the only English speaker, the only skinny, non-dancing, white woman in a community of voluptuous black bodies whose feet stepped in time to an imaginary salsa beat even when they were just heading out to do laundry.

'Gudge morning!' More women filed past as I bathed in the river, wooden paddles ready to beat their clothes on the flat stones, battering out the jungle dirt and flecks of fruit juice and chicken blood. They were proud of their new English words, and keen to practise on me. Twice a day I stood in front of the broken blackboard in the garishly painted nursery that became my classroom. The women – many breastfeeding or holding young children – squeezed into the tiny children's chairs and repeated after me, 'Welcome… to… Wimbí!'

In the evenings I created flashcards by candlelight, while Agueda brought me bread and tea. These flashcards, and drilling, were the basis of the class; literacy levels were low, and one or two of the women could not read at all. There is little need for words or books when your world revolves around logging and laundry and cooking coconut fish stew following recipes passed from grandmother to mother to daughter. And there is little time to finish school when you are pregnant with your first child at fourteen, still a child yourself. But this was not an unusual situation in this forgotten jungle province.

I understood just how significant these classes were for some community members when Fanny, a heavily pregnant mother of five, volunteered to write the answer to a question on the board. Fanny could not read or write, but she carefully reproduced the characters written in her neighbour's notebook in front of the class, with a huge smile spreading across her face. I realised these were probably the first words she had ever written – and they were in English.

Before my journey began I knew virtually nothing about Esmeraldas as it featured in no guidebooks or travel websites or forums. No-one ever went there. All I knew was that it had jungle – lots of it. This was one of the last remaining stretches of the Chocó rainforest, wedged between the Andes and the Pacific, and it sheltered monkeys, sloths, armadillos and FARC guerillas inching over the Colombian border – hence the lack of tourists. It was also home to Afro-Ecuadorians, the descendants of former African slaves and miners who had escaped or been freed several centuries ago. They had headed inland from the coast and down from the mountains and established villages along the furthest stretches of the Santiago and Cayapas rivers, in territory that could only be reached by dugout canoe. Here, far from mainstream Ecuadorian society, they maintained African customs and cuisine and superstitions. They played marimba and maracas, instruments hewn from the forest, and danced, all shuffling feet and shaking hips, to haunting vocals that originated in homelands they could not remember, but whose rhythms they still heard in their dreams.

Centuries on, daily life in the Afro-Ecuadorian village of Wimbí remained much the same. A few villagers proudly brandished mobile phones; but there was no reception, so they just tapped them, blasting out tinny ringtones. There was no running water, but the river ran day and night, cool and clear, the lifeblood of the village. Women panned for gold in the river, men fished in it. There was electricity, but the lines could be severed for days at a time – whereupon candles were brought out and generators switched on, powering stereos that pumped out salsa music into the steamy jungle night until they ran out of petrol. There was little entertainment beyond the weekly discos, the fuzzy televisions, and now the English classes. But I didn't miss what I had once considered to be life's essentials. The river was a perfectly good substitute for a shower, the candles eased the darkness, with music we could dance, and we could chat and cook and play cards.

Ironically, the one thing I did miss, desperately, was my privacy. I had assumed that loneliness would be an unavoidable part of backpacking alone across South America, but in Wimbí I ached to be lonely. I never got used to the unannounced visitors, the neighbours who walked into my home, the children rousing me from my siesta, begging me to photograph them; I never got used to the constant gossip and snooping and the fact that my business was now everyone else's. My month alone in the jungle turned out to be the most sociable month of my life – whether I wanted it to be or not. A solo traveller here would not remain one for long. There are no strangers in Wimbí.

Some students came with gifts, voluntary payment for my lessons – coconuts, homemade ice creams frozen on to splinters of wood, sticks of sweet sugarcane to suck and chew before spitting out the pulp. But the teacher-student roles were frequently reversed, and over the course of the month I learned far more than I taught.

'So, what juices will you be serving the tourists?' I asked the women.

'Coco,' came the reply.

'Coconut. OK.'

'*Maracuyá.*'

'Right – that's passionfruit.'

'Guava.'

'Err...' I was stumbling.

'*Guanábana.*'

'*Borojó.*'

'*Anona.*'

'*Tomate de árbol...*'

The list went on. I had no idea what these fruits were, and the women patiently explained in simple terms.

'It's green and yellow and it's very sweet.'

'It's white inside and soft. You have to mix it with sugar.'

They taught me, and I taught them back, how to explain these wonderful foods, the riches of their jungle, to the future tourists.

Early on, children began sitting in on the classes. The village school was unreliable, with classes cancelled at least once or twice a week. The children, like their mothers, were bored and restless; they didn't want to be left out. As they disrupted the adult classes, it was agreed that I should offer a class for the kids after lunch, when they came racing out of school. They screamed and shouted their way through the lessons, with a thirst for knowledge unknown in many Western schools. I enjoyed the fast, fun pace of these classes in contrast to the patient repetition of the adult sessions.

We moved on from 'My name is Bicki' – once they had learned to insert their own names – to colours. Rather than attempting to shout above the din, I would whisper, forcing the children to stop their yelling and hang on my every word.

As they shushed each other, I said quietly, 'Touch something… blue.'

Thirty children sprinted across the room, shrieking, and attempted to grab the large black seed I wore on a string around my neck, a handmade gift from one of the villagers.

'No,' I yelled. '*Blue!*'

They jumped on chairs, bounced across the nursery floor, touching T-shirts, tables, pencils.

'Good! Now touch something… *red!*'

They swarmed again towards my necklace, howling with joy. I sighed, defeated, and let myself be enveloped in warm, sticky hands and surrounded by laughter.

Vicki Brown caught the solo travel bug aged twelve, when she travelled, alone, to visit her Austrian penfriend. She subsequently found various ways to spend time abroad, working as a TEFL teacher, writer, photographer,  designer and painter. She has now settled in London – a city where you can encounter different cultures, languages and foods every day – which keeps her itchy feet well scratched in between travels.

The Wandering Goose
Janet Rogers

I stare out of the rain-splashed window as the bus, a bendy variety, writhes and twists through the city. The late-October dawn is peeling back grey covers allowing daylight to creep in. I see shiny black water swirling in the canal. There is an awakening in the streets. I peer into shop windows – a butcher is cutting up a carcass, a baker filling her window with apple tarts and éclairs. The city is gathering speed. I am squashed beneath a large rucksack and nudged by the bulk of an oversized French woman.

I should be at home with my husband of forty years, taking retirement at an amble, reading newspapers, breathing slowly, sitting in soft chairs. But in our house the soft chairs are undented.

My husband likes the rise and fall of a choppy sea with the wind in his sails. I like to stay on firm ground. So we decided to roam alone. I wanted to discover the real France and improve my French. I had to live and work there, as holidays were just not enough. I would be on my own and fear of the unknown made my skin prickle. As I packed my rucksack I wondered whether lurching about on a rough sea might not be so bad after all. I decided I needed to toughen up.

So here I am in a foreign land, heading for I know not exactly what or where, a farm in the Normandy countryside. I have arranged to meet a French farmer in a town. An email, anonymous and efficient, fixed the deal – a month's food and board for five hours' farm work per day and weekends free.

I'm travelling towards an organic apple farm to live with strangers. I change buses in the city centre. A strike means that I will have a three-hour wait. I wander and consume large quantities of coffee and text my host.

Now I am on the bus, speeding through country lanes. I pester the driver in my best French to let me know when I reach my destination. The thought of missing my rendezvous and racing through the French countryside forever makes my stomach churn. I swallow hard. 'If you don't like it you can always come home,' my husband said encouragingly as he waved goodbye. That's fine, but French trains and buses, I've discovered, can be unpredictable. Escaping may not be as easy as he made it sound.

I step down from the bus, unfold my body from hours of cramped travelling in train, boat and bus, hoist my rucksack on my back and look around. The rain has stopped. I am in a small, quiet town of grey stone, shuttered buildings and a few shops. A church spire pierces the dull sky.

How will the farmer recognise me? Maybe I should have mentioned that I'm not a fully paid-up member of the volunteering generation. A word about my eligibility for pensions and bus passes might have been sensible.

While I stand regretting my omission a dilapidated Citroën rattles to a halt and a woman leans across and flings open a door. 'Jeanette?'

'*Oui.*' I smile.

'Isabelle,' she says, waving a hand, then adds, '*Attends*', 'Wait', as she brushes dried mud and straw from the seat. The back of the car is piled high with straw bales and sacks of animal feed.

I climb in and immediately start to apologise. *'Je suis désolée. Je suis un peu plus âgée que vous pourriez avoir voulu,'* I splutter. 'I'm sorry. I'm a little older than you might have wished.'

It doesn't matter. She tells me any age is fine as long as I'm prepared to do 'the work'. I can see from the state of her hands – black nails and stained fingers – that she does 'the work'. Will my hands look like hers after a month, I wonder.

We bounce through a maze of narrow lanes crouched beneath high hedges and overhanging trees. We chat about my journey and the farm, mainly in French, but with some English words masquerading as French. I have been travelling for sixteen hours and the language switch in my brain is as yet un-oiled.

The sun is out now and the Normandy countryside lights up. I have failed to concentrate on the route. A trail of breadcrumbs might have helped, for when Isabelle swings the car into a stony courtyard and we pull up in front of a shuttered farmhouse, I have no idea how we got there.

It is a truly French house, grand but weary. Virginia creeper in every shade of red and orange blazes over the grey stonework. Skinny black cats laze on the wall in the autumn sunshine and a bubble of French words bursts through the open windows.

Inside the farmhouse kitchen a Rumanian guy waves from the dark recess where he is frying *galettes*, while a German girl stops chopping cabbage to shake my hand and two French teenagers, long-legged like antelopes, wave as they flit back and forth placing plates and glasses on the table. A surly young man slumped on a bench, with dreadlocks beneath a knitted hat, is less welcoming. He looks up and nods.

One of the young French girls seems to notice my unease. She grasps my arm and whispers, 'It's all right, Eban doesn't live here.'

Lunch is simple and delicious. I join in the conversation. French words, wonderful, nonchalant, harmonious words from a language which has captivated me for years, slot miraculously into my brain. Subjunctives, learned as a teenager, stumble out of dark caverns.

I look around. It is as though the room has been caught in a sand storm. A layer of dust covers every surface, clinging to bedraggled spider plants, dried herbs, bread baskets, a row of tea pots on a shelf and random piles of books and letters. On the radiator in the corner, a collection of grey tea towels moulders and in front of the wood-burning stove an ironing board sags beneath a small mountain of laundry.

Cats lurk in corners like bands of thieves waiting for their chance to steal. One has given up all pretence and is clawing at the fridge door, unaware that a wooden chair, strategically placed, will prevent it opening.

After lunch Isabelle shows me to my room. A prison cell might be more inviting and probably cleaner. My boots scrape on the gritty floorboards and cobwebs hang from the walls and ceiling. A cat is asleep on the bed. Isabelle shoves it away and promises me a clean cover.

She shows me the bathroom. There's a cracked basin, a bath and shower nursing the grime of many years and many bodies and a composting toilet with a scattering of wood shavings on the floor as evidence of the silent, waterless procedure. Grey towels hang drying on a piece of string. A dank, musty smell pervades the room.

There are trespassers in my head stalking my courage and implanting little wisps of fear. Almost imperceptible cracks of doubt are spreading in my mind with no regard for what I really feel deep down in my heart.

I retreat to the kitchen and find a broom. I sweep down the walls, ceiling and floor, put a clean cover on my bed, adjust the tattered brown curtains. Tomorrow I will clean the bathroom and shower and wash away my discomfort.

In the meantime I walk to the lake with Andrei and Magna and see the reflections of the poplar trees in the water and hear the rooks shouting in the high branches. We sit on a tree trunk and chat in French, our common language. On the way back we collect pears and walnuts and talk, also in French, to the goats in the front enclosure.

In the kitchen, as we prepare supper, I learn that it is our responsibility to save the planet.

'It is fundamental to live in harmony with nature. We must always think of the consequences of our actions,' Isabelle declares, in between issuing dictates about how to wash up using only two bowls of water, how to recycle or compost everything and when it is permissible to flick the electric light switch.

Later I sit down to supper by the light of a low-wattage bulb and watch the flies scuttle round the lampshade, casting shadows the size of mice on the walls, and a spider spinning yet another web and wonder if I am ready to live quite so harmoniously with nature.

But as the days slip by, I settle easily into the rhythm of country living. I get to know the sheep, chickens, ducks and geese and the vulgar eating habits of the Vietnamese pigs. I'm entranced by the long fluttering eyelashes of the large brown cow, chilled by the icy cross-eyed stare of the small grey mare and encouraged by the free-spirited, snow-white goose who likes nothing better than to escape from the pen and wander on her own.

I look forward to the days we spend in the orchard picking apples. I love the camaraderie of the volunteers from local farms who turn out to help, the sound of the apples thudding to the ground as they're knocked down with a pole and the scrambling and scratching on our hands and knees in the long grass, like dogs searching for bones. I love, too, the long lazy lunches and the amble back to the farmhouse, weary and warm at the end of the day, and the simple reward for our labours – tea, apple juice and slices of spicy cake, served on the terrace where we sit drinking and talking until the moon is high in the sky and the air is chilled.

I walk in the fields with Isabelle and we pick wild sorrel leaves and plantain for salad, and nettles for soup. We climb through woods under vast oak trees and slide down slopes using acorns as roller skates. We tread through boggy meadows searching for the sweet-smelling herb, queen of the meadow, to make a tisane. We pick plump sloes, hawthorn berries and hips from the wild rose to make aperitifs. I learn the French name for plants for which I have yet to discover the English equivalent.

Volunteers come and go. Neighbours pop in and chat. I meet the donkey keeper who communes with her fifteen donkeys and the sculptor who makes strange creatures from wood. Doors are never locked.

I plant a strawberry bed, clean and cook and help with groups of school children who visit the farm to learn about the animals and apple juice production. Isabelle takes them into the barn and they set to work crunching and squashing the apples, allowing the juice to run out, filling jugs and bottles with the golden nectar

On my last evening a neighbour holds a farewell soirée for me. We sit around a little table and eat crudités and pâté on morsels of bread. We drink *prunelle*, a sweet liqueur distilled from plums, and a sour drink made with gentian flowers and listen to Bob Dylan singing 'The Times They Are A-Changin''.

Afterwards, as night falls and the moon rises, I must return to the farm to pack my rucksack. But first I go in search of the wandering goose. I find her in the hedgerow beneath the sycamore trees. I scoop her up, stroke her long silky neck and look into her gentle eyes and praise her for her courage, then return her to the pen.

Janet Rogers worked as a news reporter in her twenties, returning to writing when she retired. She has won several national travel-writing competitions and her articles have appeared in the UK and Australian press. She is a keen cyclist and swimmer and did her first triathlon aged seventy. She lives by the sea in West Sussex.

The Pet Project

Jennifer Barclay

I didn't really stop crying until I was halfway around the world.

I had left my best friend, Lisa, at home in Greece. Lisa the Labrador-cross was my affectionate furry girl, my constant canine companion. We scrambled over mountains together, took long walks to beaches and swam in the sea, returning home to curl up on the couch. I couldn't put her through the flight and quarantine to bring her with me on a trip I knew would be temporary, a year or less. I ensured she would be well looked after while I was away. But I was devastated to leave her and travel solo to Australia.

I'd never particularly wanted to travel to Australia. It was a calculated risk to follow Ian to New South Wales where he'd recently begun looking after his mother, after she was diagnosed with dementia. We were newly in love, idealistic – and we completely underestimated how tough it would be. In a dull suburban house, with a woman who didn't understand why I was there and a man who felt helpless to make things better, after a couple of very difficult months I started to dream of home and the easy companionship of my dog.

But thinking of Lisa gave me an idea. I signed up to an Australian website as a pet-sitter, where you care for someone's animals in return for a free place to stay. It was my – our – salvation, though it meant that in the pursuit of love, I'd reluctantly have to travel solo once again.

As I sat in the passenger seat of the car en route to my assignment, a scruffy white terrier called Major redefined pet-sitting clearly by jumping on my lap. Major was a living rendition of the tail wagging the dog. He pined a little after his owner left for Bali, then I took him for a walk and his ears flapped up and down with excitement as he trotted along. Dogs have simple needs, and once you prove you know where the food's kept and where they like to pee, they can breathe easy.

All of a sudden, I had some breathing space too.

Rays of sunlight streamed on to my bed and I heard the strange whistles of magpies and rough caw of cockatoos. On the northern edge of Katoomba in the Blue Mountains, the wood-and-stone house flowed down the slope of the hill, with tall windows opening directly on to the bush. I sat outside on the deck to eat my toast. Walking Major later, I found a nature reserve and, just off the trail, stopped at a creek where the ripples reflected on an overhanging tree and dappled it with light. Gradually a canyon opened up, and down below were trees, tangled and unkempt and magical, and a narrow cataract of water falling from a mossy ledge down to a green pool. I was thrilled; it was the first time I'd discovered things on my own since coming to Australia.

Ian visited for a few days, and I took him there. We jumped into the deep water, icy but exhilarating, swimming across to be pummelled by water cascading from the cliffs before dashing back to dry off in the sun on the rocks. I was at a waterhole in the Blue Mountains, I thought, and if I hadn't come pet-sitting, I might never have done this. Travelling alone was already restoring my equilibrium, my confidence and sense of self.

After Ian left, I missed him, but I took a train a few stops up the line to Mount Victoria, and walked alone among the big trees on a path overgrown with bush and ferns, jumping at the thought of snakes every time a leaf moved. Again I spent a childishly happy half hour in a private waterfall in the wilderness. On a Friday night at Katoomba's Station Bar I found a local musician playing his own bluegrass songs on steel guitar, his mouth organ sounding like a train passing through the mountains. I smiled and chatted with people, far away from the sadness of a month ago. A tall, skinny guy said I should get up to dance, so I did. I laughed and danced, and didn't want the music to end.

It was the start of an adventure, finding assignments that helped me discover New South Wales – and naturally I discovered things about myself, too. My next assignment took me many hours south, to eleven remote acres. Arriving after a day on the bus, I sat on the back steps and poured a glass of Tempranillo from the box, looking out over green hills reaching off into the distance. The sunset glinted off the many windows of the house, four old portable school classrooms joined together by wooden walkways, like the carriages of a train. In veering towards rural settings, I wondered if I'd bitten off more than I could chew. I had to look after two dogs, two goats, a dozen hens with chicks and a handful of cats; to get into town, I'd have to learn to drive the ute. But with a bouncy Labrador under one arm and a wriggly border collie under the other, I wouldn't be lonely.

Over the next few months I would alternate between time on my own, and snatching a few days with Ian (and Ann). Ann was always excited about the idea of going on holiday, and if she was confused by all my houses, better to be confused somewhere with stimulation and entertainment than in her own home in front of the telly. Her family noticed how much happier she was. I got used to the sight of them arriving – tiny Ann in her best outfit and hat, Ian tall and towering over her, dazed from a trying journey and bewildered that all this was happening. At least, with all the enforced time apart, we were always happy to see one another.

In between, I looked after dogs and cats, sheep and a python, hens and ducks. Back home, with Lisa, I'd never have been able to do this. I met some interesting people, and got close to lots of animals, pets and otherwise. I saw goannas and blue-tongued lizards, walked among wallabies and kangaroos. And for December, I arranged for Ian and Ann to join me at a cabin in the woods by the ocean where I was cat-sitting.

For the first week or two, Ann loved being somewhere pretty and different, eating ice cream in the park and watching old films in the afternoon. Then one day, she decided she was going home, and Ian thought it best that I drive them back. It was easier for him to look after her at home, he said. The stress of driving the coastal highway amid busy, fast holiday traffic poured out of me in gallons of tears when we arrived back at Ann's house. Not only would I be on my own for Christmas with two grumpy cats – I had assignments lined up for months and I had no idea when I would see Ian again. I pulled myself together, got in the car and drove away, angry and frustrated.

But every mile felt good. It was easier alone, and at least I was free. We'd given Ian's mum some happy times, and should be proud of that. And I'd never forget the places I'd stayed and the animals I'd met. The countryside as I drove south was all thick green grass and big old trees. Eventually I turned off the highway and breathed a sigh of relief to slow down at the 'All roads in Dalmeny 50' sign. I smiled to see the glinting water of the inlet, and on a whim I turned into a parking spot by the ocean. I'd always wanted to have fish and chips there but we'd never gone, as Ann didn't like fish. As I waited for my barramundi, the young lad from the shop asked, 'Seen the emus yet?' I ate outside in the cool, soft breeze and I couldn't remember ever enjoying fish and chips so much.

It's possible that when I returned to Greece, Lisa noticed the hairs and smells of a dozen strange dogs on me. But she was too polite to say so.

Jennifer Barclay grew up in a village in the hills in the north of England and has written several books including *Meeting Mr Kim*, *Falling in Honey* and *An Octopus in my Ouzo*. She lives on a Greek island and works remotely with other people's books, occasionally writing articles for newspapers or magazines, and blogs at www.octopus-in-my-ouzo. blogspot.com.

Doing a Shirley Valentine
Christine Green

People travel alone for many reasons, and my introduction to going solo arose from exhaustion after a couple of hectic months lambing six hundred ewes on our small farm.

'Why not have a week in the sun?' my husband suggested, and as the March rain lashed down this prospect seemed very tempting. But as I scanned the sheep pens during my time on duty in the lambing shed, my mind was full of doubts. I wondered whose hand I would grab if the plane hit a patch of turbulent air. And what about my fear of landing? How would I occupy each day? How would I feel eating on my own? Would there be language difficulties? How would my family manage at home without me, with all the farm work?

I reflected. This wasn't something I *had* to do. Some people had no option but to travel on their own. They coped, so why did I have so many misgivings? I had the blessing and encouragement from my family. My daughter even bought me a video of *Shirley Valentine*, the story that's probably been responsible for many ladies going on holiday alone. I think she envisaged me having a fling in the sun with Tom Conti.

In the days before the internet and instant communications, things were far more uncertain. I booked a package holiday, which provided assurance against things going wrong; and I decided upon

Mallorca because we had been there years before, so simple things like arriving at the airport would be familiar. I knew, however, that much as I enjoyed reading, I would soon tire of lying on a beach all day; I would also need company. My main hobby was hillwalking so I chose the scenic northern part of the island which I knew about from walking magazines. It was with great trepidation, all the same, that I left my family of two teenagers and husband to fend for themselves. Deposited outside the airport terminal, it felt very odd to be on my own for the first time in many years.

In a farming community it certainly wasn't 'done' for the farmer's wife to go off on her own, especially after lambing with the ewes and their lambs to be attended to, fed, counted and so on. I believe some tongues wagged. Had we fallen out and had I really staged a *Shirley Valentine*? We were, though, no ordinary farming family. My husband, a chartered accountant with his own practice, had never had any interest in golf and had long hung up his rugby boots. Instead his love had always been sheep. Starting with twelve sheep as a hobby, we had somehow ended up buying a farm and increasing our flock to six hundred breeding ewes. This hobby was combined with office work, so quite often I was left holding the fort on the farm.

You've earned this rest, I told myself as I mingled with families and couples in the airport lounge. Still, doubts crossed my mind. My consolation lay in my walking boots, because I knew that if I could link up with a walking group I would be doing something I loved with like-minded people.

I arrived at a small hotel at the head of Pollença Bay. It really was a *Shirley Valentine* moment to have left a rainy Cardiff, soggy sheep and muddy fields and within three hours gaze over the sparkling blue water, feel the heat envelop me and reflect that this must surely be paradise. Missing in paradise was my husband to hand me my first drink and to clink glasses to our holiday. This lonely feeling, on the moment of arrival, has never left me during the years which followed any time I ventured off on my own. However, with new surroundings, new smells and the warmth of a different climate, such feelings were soon dispelled and I rose to the challenge of my adventure.

I had chosen a smaller hotel rather than a big impersonal one thinking that it was easier to become lonely in a crowd. This proved to be true, because by evening I was already chatting with other residents, and I quickly found that I was not the only person travelling alone.

The following morning I made my way into the town to locate the walking group. A former representative of a travel company had recently set up his own walking holiday company. I was shown a list of the week's walks on offer. The system was that you added your name, chose your walk and indicated if you needed collecting by the minibus or preferred to meet at the bus station. I already had my Sunflower guidebook with me, so I soon decided that a day's circuit around Valldemossa was right up my street, and enrolled for the walk the following day.

I was surprised at how comfortable I felt strolling around on my own. With no decisions to be made except how I would fill the empty day ahead of me, I headed for the beach, lay down on the warm sand, got out my book and soon forgot about everything else. Now, with instant mobile communications, one could be checking on news and weather or emailing friends and family, but twenty-five years ago travelling abroad on one's own was an adventure. Contact with family was restricted to landline telephone calls, which made the experience more profound.

Although I had been looking forward to my day in the mountains, new worries assailed me as I began to doubt my ability to cope with the walk which was described as including 'strenuous ascents of 2,625 feet' and deemed 'suitable for experienced walkers who do not suffer from vertigo'. Fortunately, the Brecon Beacons had been a good training ground and I need not have worried. Soon I had made friends with my fellow walkers who came from a broad range of ages and circumstances all over the UK. In my guidebook I noted: 'Good ridge walk, v.v. rocky descent.'

Richard, the group leader, hosted a weekly promotional evening in one of the resort's big hotels. Suddenly I was in good company, a glass of sangria to hand, and, through the slide show, was transported around this magical island. Mallorca was a magnet for cyclists as well as walkers. The hotel was buzzing with people who were drawn together for all sorts of reasons. It did not matter that I had travelled alone. Since that brief moment on arrival at my hotel, I had never felt alone, or lonely.

The rest of the week was spent with further walking, day trips, sunbathing and swimming. The lambing shed seemed on another planet and, by the end of my week, I was ready to return to family life.

This was the first of what became known as my 'post-lambing pick-me-ups'. From being looked at askance by some of the farming fraternity, I became an object of envy. I could go off on my own, enjoy myself and simply pick up the reins when I returned. 'How do you do it?' I was often asked. The truth is that my health benefited from my travelling. My husband always says that it is a joy to welcome me home looking so relaxed and tanned. I joke that I have to go abroad for medicinal reasons. Do we not all feel so much better in the winters and chilly springs if we have spent some time in the sun? I always return refreshed and renewed.

As both our flock and my mountain walking have decreased, my interest in painting has taken over. Five years ago I decided that I would combine some spring sun with a painting course. A search on the internet led me to the beautiful home of an international artist living near Pollença, and so my love affair with Mallorca has continued. I did not fall for a Tom Conti, but I did fall in love with Mallorca, and the affair continues into my seventieth year.

Christine Green lives with her husband on a small sheep farm near Monmouth, and is mostly involved with the flock during lambing. Her interests include reading, painting, Pilates and swimming and she is planning to cycle from Land's End to John O'Groats. She enjoys the company of her family and two grandchildren.

Tips

A small guesthouse run by a family who look out for you can be safer than a big, anonymous hotel. *Claire Davies*

Link your travel to your interest, be it architecture, painting, bridge or whatever. Through this you will enjoy some good company which will enhance your experience. *Christine Green*

Take a sketch book – it doesn't matter whether you're a good artist or not, but it's a great excuse for sitting and staring. Think up some research project to give you a focus. Or set yourself the task of reading one or two of those books you've always meant to read but haven't found the time. *Elspeth Cardy*

Sitting in a bar or restaurant to read a newspaper early in the evening can get you into a colourful conversation. *Jennifer Barclay*

Research the main scams of a country and be ready if necessary to dismiss overly friendly people at tourist sites. *Matt Dawson*

Connecting

Connecting is more than a brief encounter, it's spending enough time with someone to feel that you have become friends. Michelle Kennedy explains: 'Yes, you choose the destination on your own, make the plans on your own, board the aeroplane on your own; but once you arrive at your destination you find yourself among the people who live there, not to mention various fellow travellers. If you are travelling solo, you are much more likely to meet them.' Matthew Pointon's connection on holiday in Norway leads him to visit the grave of someone he's seen only fleetingly. Suzy Pope survives sub-zero Mongolia with a gradually thawing South African while Gillian Gain warms to the American way of life, despite their unnerving love of guns. Finally, a much slower connection: Mollie the pony is more consistently negative about travelling solo than any contributor to this book.

First Night

Michelle Kennedy

I anxiously surveyed the crowd of faces in anticipation. Eyes lit up, smiles broadened, cries of joy went up. None were for me. No familiar face in the crowd. He had promised to be here. My eyes finally descended on a slight man with a moustache, wearing a dirty brown shirt and dirtier brown trousers, who held a sign written in blue marker: 'Mr Michelle Jennedy'. This was apparently as much of a welcome as I was going to get.

He didn't speak to me, but motioned for me to follow and led me outside to a bus. No sooner had I taken an aisle seat so as not to have to share, than a man came and asked if the window seat next to me was free. I was immediately on guard. There were still plenty of other seats free. *Oh no*, I thought, *I've barely set foot in the country and it's already begun.*

I had been warned by fellow travellers about Indian men – that they could be brazenly forward, that I should have lies about 'my husband' prepared ahead of time, that I should be ready to slap them. But before I could do any of this, some other part of my brain acted and I politely offered up the seat. I sat stiffly for the next few minutes, surveying him out of the corner of my eye, wondering if I could actually slap someone.

He seemed harmless. He was dressed in a suit and a button-down shirt and tie, his hair thinning, a pair of wire-rimmed rectangular glasses hooked over his nose. He looked crumpled, as if he too had just stepped off a long-haul flight. He could have been a middle-aged businessman anywhere, really.

I started to relax. Then the conductor came by.

'Where are you going, madam?'

'Pune.'

He looked at me blankly.

'Yes. Where?'

'I don't know. Pune. Don't *you* know?' I assumed the person who'd met me with a sign knew where I was going.

At this point, the man beside me entered the conversation, insisting that the conductor must ask the driver to check if the booking office had provided an address where I was to be dropped off.

'How is it you don't know where you are going?' he then asked, turning to me. 'And why are you travelling alone?'

It was not actually my intention to travel alone. I had toured for a few months alone around Europe, sure, but India was different. I had been led to believe by those around me that travelling in India as a single female in my twenties was beyond my capacity, possibly even dangerous. My boyfriend had travelled in India many times. His parents were Indian and he could speak passable Hindi. So we decided that he would meet me upon my arrival in Mumbai and we would travel together for the next few months. Already, as we planned our trip, I sensed from the way he spoke ('always travel in first class AC trains', 'only take tourist class buses') that my experience in India was going to pass through the filter of how he saw things. He had experienced discomfort, unbelievable delays and unexpected events on Indian trains and now he had no tolerance for any of it.

I felt uneasy about this. I wanted the whole experience of travel in India, not just the comfortable and convenient one on air-conditioned trains, where everything goes to plan. Yet I felt unable to assert myself. After all, I had never been to India. Maybe it really was a difficult place for a woman to travel. I was young, an inexperienced traveller, and I doubted my own ability to work things out. And so I agreed to follow.

He would meet me at the airport in Mumbai. That's what his last email had said. The airport greeting was a far cry from the passionate embrace I had been expecting after several months apart. Neither of us had a mobile phone. I had no idea where he was staying in Pune. It hadn't occurred to me to ask. In fact, I knew very little about Pune at all. The way he talked about it, it sounded small, though now, consulting the Lonely Planet as I sat on the bus, my naivety regarding Indian travel was confirmed – it turned out Pune was the second-largest city in Maharashtra, with a population of over five million, not a small village where you just roll up and ask if anyone's seen a Canadian. A mild sense of panic began to overtake my confusion. What was I going to do? Why was he not there?

The man beside me looked at me with concern. I had the acute sense that this was no longer my problem. It was our problem. Or possibly, his problem. It certainly felt out of my hands.

He started discussing the situation with a man seated across the aisle. If the driver didn't have the address of my boyfriend's hotel, what then? After much debate, it was decided that, being Canadian, my boyfriend would be staying in one of the better hotels, probably somewhere near the Osho Meditation Resort. They agreed to split up the phone numbers and try calling them from the rest stop, halfway between Mumbai and Pune. Having found a solution to my problem for the immediate future, the man turned to me to introduce himself.

'I am Sujay Godbole. I have just flown in from Swiss.' He then went on to explain that he had been working on an IT contract in Zurich for the past six months, and was on his way home to spend the Christmas holidays with his family.

I told him that I was taking a belated gap year. I had completed my master's degree and started working, only to decide to take the year out to explore other sides of myself, while exploring other sides of the world. So far I had walked across Spain and visited France and Portugal. India felt like the largest leap in terms of change of culture. I had been travelling for over twelve hours and was suffering from jet lag. At that moment, I felt more tired than worried about where I was going to sleep that night. After all, I could sleep right here on the bus. And I did.

Sujay woke me up at the rest stop. He disappeared, and then reappeared, two cups of *chai* in hand.

'We have tried the hotels,' he said, 'but they do not have a booking in his name.'

Later, back on the bus, he gently asked me what I was planning to do. I didn't really have a plan. I told him I would ask to be dropped at the bus station and hope that my boyfriend would be waiting there. It would be impossible to find a guesthouse at this time of night. And anyway it would only be a few hours until daybreak. If my boyfriend wasn't there, I would just have to wait. Surely he would then come to look for me in the morning.

'Or,' said Sujay, 'there is another possibility. You could come and stay at my parents' place.'

I looked over at him. This was not a man I would need to slap, I thought. But there possibly would be some near the bus station at 3 a.m.

I have no idea what passed through the minds of his family when, some hours later, Sujay showed up with a young and dishevelled North American backpacker. They greeted me warmly, however, and his mother made me a bed in the sitting room. Though in the back of my mind I worried about my boyfriend being worried, I was soon fast asleep.

In the morning, I was properly introduced to Sujay's wife, and his mother and father, and his six-year-old son, Asim. I ate my first Indian breakfast – spicy flaked rice with vegetables and several cups of chai. Later, I took my first rickshaw ride, with Sujay, to the European part of town, and found my boyfriend at the first café we walked into. He told me he had been frantically calling the bus company and emailing me all morning, trying to find me. He looked relieved, both to see me there safe, and to see that I didn't look angry. It turned out the bus company had lost the address details he had given them when he made the booking. Their mistake had let me make my first friends in India, on my own, no guide required.

As it happened, my boyfriend was called back home on business a few weeks later. This left me to discover India on my own, not through his filter or anyone else's. I travelled every class of train carriage there was, and found that first class AC was the one I liked the least, and where I felt the most vulnerable as a woman because the cars isolate you more from other people. I discovered that in second class and, even better, in sleeper class, people talked with each other more, shared food and looked out for one another; while in sleeper class you can open the windows and see the countryside much better. I discovered that I too can learn enough Hindi to direct a rickshaw driver, that I can drive a hard bargain in the market, work out where to go next and how to get there, get lost and find the way again, choose good hotels and hotels with bedbugs. I learned to tell the difference between my own self-doubt and the fears of others, and to not let my decisions be guided by either. I learned that there are many ways to travel, and had the chance to find my own way, and be my own guide.

The story of my arrival in India sounded unbelievable to many Westerners I met, but for me the essentials of the experience were repeated throughout my six-month solo journey through the country. In every corner of India I met with kindness. I met interesting people who were interested in me. I rarely felt alone and found help whenever it was needed. Best of all, I spent much of my time with Indian people.

I attended a four-day wedding in Gujarat, as a guest of the groom's family. The women put kohl around my eyes and bangles on my wrists. The children taught me traditional Dandiya dances, which require not just coordination of your feet, but also the ability to knock sticks together with the people beside you. I rode side-saddle on the back of a motorbike loaded down with firewood, to visit a farm in Tamil Nadu. The farmer's wife milked their cow, boiled the milk and then spent ages pouring it between two cups to cool it, so I would not burn my tongue when I tasted it; while the farmer's children taught me the words for cow and milk in Tamil. I was cared for by a kind Tibetan nurse when I came down with dysentery upon arriving in Dharamsala. She stopped by my guesthouse room over the course of several days, bringing me boiled water and plain rice when I was able to eat again.

One thing people never mention about solo travel is that solo does not necessarily mean alone. Yes, you choose the destination on your own, make your plans on your own and board the aeroplane on your own; but once you arrive at your destination you find yourself among the people who live there, not to mention various fellow travellers. If you are travelling solo, you are much more likely to meet them.

Michelle Kennedy (aka Satwant Kaur) is a speech therapist and Kundalini yoga teacher. She grew up in northern British Columbia, Canada, and left to travel the world  at twenty-seven. She now lives in London. Her most recent trips have included a five hundred-kilometre walk through France on the Chemin de St Jacques and a stint studying Raag and Gurmukhi in Amritsar, India.

A Sack of Beans and a Sun-Bleached Chair

Mandy Huggins

The shady terrace at Casa Mendales looks out towards the ocean across the mismatched rooftops and patch-pocket gardens of Cojímar. This sleepy Cuban fishing town languishes beneath a sky of washday blue, and the sand-dusted road shimmers with midday mirages.

Cojímar is famous as the place where Hemingway came to fish, and where he met Anselmo Hernández, the fisherman who was immortalised in *The Old Man and the Sea*. Day trippers come from far and wide to visit La Terraza bar, with its beguiling setting at the water's edge. From Hemingway's favourite table you can watch the fishing boats heading out to sea, and feel his ghost in the cool breeze that blows through the open window.

Everyone here has an anecdote to tell about Hemingway, or claims to be related to Hernández, and my host, Tanya, is no exception – Hernández, she claims, was a distant cousin.

Tanya Mendales is the larger-than-life owner of my *casa particular*. She sits next to me on the terrace among pots of sunflowers, painting her nails a startling orange. On the street below, two women sashay past with their dachshund, his coat as shiny as a newly opened conker. Tanya leans precariously over the rusty railing and shouts down to them. The women roar with infectious laughter, flashing bright white smiles. My Spanish is not good enough to catch what they are saying, but their laughter needs no translation.

I feel so at ease here with Tanya that it seems like a lifetime ago that I arrived at Havana airport, feeling more than a little apprehensive. I decided to make this trip alone on the spur of the moment. Cuba had been at the top of my list for years, but none of my potential travelling companions even had it on theirs, and the perennial cry of 'see it before it changes' had recently become more urgent. Although I'm quite well-travelled, this is my inaugural solo long-haul trip, and my first instinct was to book a tour – safety in sightseeing-by-numbers. But a friend of a friend recommended Casa Mendales and I was soon persuaded that this was the only way to see the 'real' Cuba.

When I arrived at the airport, I waited nervously while an official tutted over my visa and accommodation details, and in baggage reclaim I eyed up my fellow passengers from the Heathrow flight. As they hauled their cases off the carousel I noticed a few with a familiar label attached. A sudden fear of the unknown made me long for the security of an air-conditioned minibus, and instilled in me a desire to rattle along the bumpy Cuban roads with the Kuoni crew. However, when I stepped outside into the bright jangle of the afternoon I was immediately greeted by a wide smile and a card bearing my name. And it was my transport that inspired envy rather than the Kuoni bus, as I was driven away by my private driver in a sleek, emerald-green 1960s Chevrolet.

Tanya and Ermano were waiting for me at the house, positioned on either side of the door in two rattan chairs, immediately welcoming and keen to put me at ease. There were ice-cold mojitos lined up, and

I was shown straight to my room in case I wanted to freshen up. The couple rent out three rooms, but I was the only guest this week, which meant I got the bathroom to myself. There were no luxuries in my room – just a single bed, a table and chair, a bright rag rug on the yellow-tiled floor and a clothes rail. The room was cool from the evening sea breeze, and there was an elderly electric fan in the corner for when things heated up – though Tanya urged me to use it 'only when very, very hot'.

As I unpacked I felt a sudden wave of homesickness, but when I pulled aside the muslin curtains I found a tiny balcony looking out towards the sea and heard Tanya's laughter drifting up from below. The sound was oddly reassuring, and just as suddenly I decided that everything about this trip would be fine. I left the rest of my unpacking for later, and headed downstairs for an ice-breaking mojito.

The Mendales both speak good English, particularly Tanya, who is a part-time teacher. Ermano is a fisherman, and spends the afternoons helping one of their neighbours in his wood-carving business. They have a car – a splendidly pimped lilac Lada with tinted windows – and they are only too happy to drive me around and show me the sights. I assure them I'm happy whiling away the hours on the terrace, writing in my notebook as I watch the colourful world go by, or walking down to the pier to watch the fishermen mend their nets. However, the chance of a trip to Hemingway's erstwhile home, Finca Vigía, is too good to turn down.

The house is set atop a hill, and is captivating. It is filled with glorious light, the rooms lined with endless bookshelves, artwork and hunting trophies. Visitors are restricted to peering through the open windows, and the resulting sense of voyeurism makes the experience all the more poignant. It is as though Hemingway may step back into the room at any moment – as he always intended to do – and pour himself a drink from the table still arranged with his original liquor bottles, or sit down to write at his sweeping curved desk.

After a simple lunch in a roadside café we drive further into the countryside to Ermano's sister's house. We pass a rugged *vaquero* – a cowboy with a handsome moustache and a dusty felt hat tipped low, seated astride a dappled mare, and leading a long-legged colt. The colt shies, and he tightens the rope. For a second our eyes meet, his expression inscrutable.

The main road is populated by as many horse carts, cowboys and bicycles as it is by cars. Speed appears to be dictated by the heat of the sun, and no-one is in a hurry. The Russian-built carriageways are straddled by crumbling bridges that lead to nowhere.

'The money ran out,' says Tanya, shrugging.

The bridges now serve an alternative purpose, providing shade from the sun for locals waiting for a lift. With fuel in short supply, they rely on a government car-share system.

I suggest to Ermano that it would be truer to the spirit of the revolution if all the half-filled tourist buses stopped for passengers too.

'We will ask Fidel to arrange it!' he says, nodding enthusiastically.

Our visit to Ermano's sister is for a special dress fitting for his niece, Angella. She is almost fifteen, and will soon be celebrating this important birthday with a traditional *quinceañera* party. Tanya has designed and made the lavish white dress that Angella will wear to parade around town. She twitches impatiently as her aunt pins the seams, and shows me the fashion magazines that were left behind at the hotel where she works. She gazes wistfully at a well-thumbed picture of a Versace dress.

Restrictions mean exploring alternative possibilities, and while Tanya conjures up new dress designs, re-using old fabrics wherever she can, Ermano grows fruit and vegetables in his *huerto*, or kitchen garden, which he sells alongside his fish. That afternoon I pick tomatoes and lettuce from the huerto with Tanya. She tells me that nearly half the vegetables in Cuba are grown either in these tiny plots or else in the larger urban co-operative gardens.

As I help prepare dinner on my last night at the Mendales home, I watch Tanya as she sweeps the floor with a rough broom, singing softly to herself. When dusk falls we carry food out on to the terrace – fresh fish, cooked with limes, accompanied by generous plates of rice. As we sip mojitos prepared with home-grown mint, I suddenly yearn for this deceptively simple life – a sack of beans, a sun-bleached chair. I feel as if I have come home. But I know that my romantic notion of a modest life is not the same as living it day in, day out, through necessity. Ermano smiles at my dream, and confirms something that I have always suspected.

'The endurance of our revolution? Maybe because we have the sun...'

'And the music?' I suggest.

Over the years, from here in Cojímar many young Cubans have attempted to sail across the Straits of Florida on homemade rafts, to follow their own dream of a better life. Ermano's nephew was one of them. He disappeared with four friends one night in 1994, and was never seen again. As Ermano finishes telling the story, we fall silent for a moment, divided by our different worlds.

Then Tanya jumps out of her chair and turns the radio up, and without hesitation she reaches out her hand to me and pulls me up to dance. The rum has worn the edges off any awkwardness I might normally feel, and just as quickly as we were divided we are united again, in a shared world of music that needs no translation.

The next morning they drive me back to Havana for a final four-night stay at the Hotel Nacional de Cuba. It's a strange and hurried goodbye, as other cars pull up behind us at the entrance and soon become impatient, but I can see Tanya's arm waving from the open window until they disappear from view at the end of the long driveway.

For a moment I feel bereft. Before I arrived in Cuba I had envisaged enjoying this part of the trip the most. I thought it would be the safe part that I would feel most comfortable with, but now the bustle of the hotel, the city, and the presence of so many Western tourists, all seem discordant and jarring. The Nacional is a famous Havana landmark and boasts a list of famous guests, from Sinatra and Sartre to Putin and Paris Hilton. But in the lobby I catch a glimpse of the sleazy side of modern-day tourism, as young Cuban boys gather to sip champagne with their older Canadian male companions, and I already miss the pastel houses and fishing boats of sleepy Cojímar, and the laughter at Casa Mendales.

I have already arranged a couple of city tours to keep me occupied for the next two days. My tour buddies are just back from the beach resort of Varadero. I recognise a couple of them from my flight. Together with our charming guide, we explore Havana. When I attune to the city I find I love it, and the group are good company. They have bonded over various mishaps and amusing incidents over the last eleven days and are now sharing the resultant in-jokes. They've had a great trip, and there's no doubt I'd have enjoyed myself if I'd toured with them, although my memories would have been totally different.

When you travel with others you still have one foot in your life at home. It's true that on your own you have no-one to share the great views with, no-one to turn to and say 'Wow!' and no-one to confer with when you're reading the map. But the compensations are worth it. On your own you get the unique chance to immerse yourself fully in the place, to truly live like a local. I already know which memories I'll treasure most – the sea breeze on my face in the early evening, the cool tiles beneath my bare feet, the taste of an ice-cold mojito infused with home-grown mint and the joy of sharing a simple meal under the stars with new friends.

Mandy Huggins lives in Yorkshire and works in engineering. Her travel writing and short fiction have won several awards and she has been placed and shortlisted in numerous other competitions including Bare Fiction, Ink Tears, Cinnamon Press, Fish and Bradt/*Independent on Sunday*. She won the British Guild of Travel Writers' New Writer Award in 2014 and was runner-up in the 2016 Dragonfly Tea/Henley Literary Festival Short Story Prize.

Alf

Matthew Pointon

The showers were communal, the coffee machine expensive, and it was right in the heart of the red-light district. But it was by far the cheapest place to stay. And, with the benefit of hindsight, it was the Sentrum Hostel that made my trip to Oslo memorable.

They say one of the advantages of travelling alone is having greater freedom in what you can do and see; but one of the downsides is the fact that you pay more for a hotel room, where the price is often the same for a single as a double. 'You'll be occupying the same room, see?' That's not so much of a problem in the developing world where rooms often cost small change anyway, but in certain countries in other parts of the world it can be a problem. And Norway is definitely one of those countries.

If I'd been with a friend or partner, they'd have probably refused to stay in a dive in the dodgiest district in town, especially once they saw the place. They'd have talked some sense into me. In fact, if sharing a room, I'd have never even considered it. But when you're alone, there is no-one to temper your drive to choose the cheapest option possible.

For the convenience of their guests, the Sentrum Hostel provided a computer for technophobes like me who lacked an iPhone. It was old, it was slow, it was dusty and it was located by the reception office. It also had someone on it. So I went and had a chat to the receptionist who was watching his national team fail to qualify for the World Cup. The guy on the computer had not moved when the game finished and so we moved on to the topic of Scandi Noir as I'd just enjoyed a meal in the restaurant where Jo Nesbø's detective Harry Hole always dines.

'I've never read the books,' said the guy, 'but he's used this hotel in some of them. They sometimes do Jo Nesbø tours and they always stop here.'

'Really?'

'Yeah, a group of people come round and take photos and stuff.'

'Why did he use this hotel?'

'Because all his books are about the Oslo underworld and half of the guests here are prostitutes.'

Aha, another reason why this place was cut-price by Norwegian standards.

'You can look it all up on the internet you know.'

'I'd like to, but... there's a guest on the computer. He's been there a while.'

'A guest? No, that's not a guest, it is Alf. Tell him to move.'

'Alf?'

'Yeah, he lives here. Sort of. Hey Alf, can you let this guy on the computer?'

Alf was a middle-aged man with a beard. He nodded and began to get up but looked unhappy, as though I was tearing him away from something important. 'Listen,' I said, 'if you need more time, I don't mind. How long do you need to finish off? I can come back.'

'Can you give me fifteen minutes?'

'Sure.'

I returned a quarter of an hour later and went on the computer, but Alf didn't leave. Instead we got chatting. That happens when you're alone. When there's another person with you it's as if people have to be invited into a party that's already started, but when there's just one it's cool. Alf was cool. He did live in the hostel. Well, sort of. He was a post-graduate student at the university. The hostel was cheaper than student accommodation. Plus he liked to meet people and talk to them. Like me. So we talked. He told me all about psychology and philosophy and we drank wine. At three I went to bed. He got back on the computer. 'I'm a night owl,' he explained.

And so that was it. I went to Oslo, saw the sights and made a friend. The end. Except that it wasn't because one of the great joys of travel is that it stays with you. And in this case, Alf did. He friended me on Facebook and continued his late-night musings on psychology, politics and non-league football. We had stuff in common that I never could have imagined. Like the fact that my local MP had once bought him a pint when he was at a conference in London. 'Nice guy,' Alf told me. 'Man's a bigoted dinosaur who can't even be bothered to live in his constituency,' I replied. Oh well, you can't agree on everything.

Sadly, several months later, he sent me a message saying that he was devastated. A friend had been murdered. She was one of the prostitutes who lived in the hosel and a customer had stabbed her in his car. Alf showed me the pictures of her and a shiver passed through me. I'd met her... briefly. She'd passed my room, wrapped in a towel, and smiled. I'd smiled back. She seemed sweet. 'She was sweet,' said Alf, 'a real sunbeam.' Now, however, she was gone.

That's travel, you know. It throws you together with people whom you'd never normally meet, gives you a glimpse into their lives, lives lived miles away and totally different. Sometimes it's just a smile; other times it's something more substantial. Always it is an experience.

The newspaper article that Alf sent me stated that the woman came originally from Dobrich in Bulgaria. Another coincidence – I was due to visit there in a few months' time. 'I should like to pay my respects at her grave,' said Alf.

'I can do it for you if you like?' I replied.

My trip to Bulgaria was not made alone. My son and a friend accompanied me and we got a far better accommodation deal. But when I went to the cemetery, stood by her grave and laid upon it a note from Alf and some flowers, I did it alone.

Some journeys have to be made that way.

Matthew Pointon is a trade unionist from Stoke-on-Trent and his two passions in life are travelling and writing. He began travelling independently in 1997 when he headed out to volunteer on  an Israeli kibbutz. After that he was hooked. His writing began in 2000 and since then he's written fiction and travelogues continuously. He's currently doing an MA in creative writing and planning his next trip – a return to North Korea! He usually travels solo although his son is tagging along more and more.

Guns and Canyons
Gillian Gain

After my husband died I thought my travelling days were finished. Being quite crippled with arthritis, travelling alone seemed too challenging.

Friends persuaded me to go on a cruise, where one is never alone, and yet I never felt more so. Because of my disability I was omitted from the lifeboat drill and there was very little help with finding my way round the ship. I eventually found the dining room and was placed at a table with other couples who had all sailed with the company previously and busily chatted about their experiences. I felt rather like the poor relation. Later, I found myself at a table of singles, however, which was better. I had to make an effort to go to the various activities on board and, luckily, I met a couple of Americans at the daily quiz. By the end of the cruise we had become so friendly that they invited me to stay with them in New Mexico.

'We collect people from all over the world,' they said. 'We are ex-military and have travelled everywhere, but we don't know our own state that well. It would be fun to visit all the canyons with you. Come next year.'

It was an exciting proposition, especially as they promised to take me to all the famous canyons I had never previously visited. I had been to the Grand Canyon with my husband, but never to Bryce, Zion, Arches,

Monument Valley, Lake Powell or the Mesa Verde. And Mal and Cat lived in Rio Rancho, a town near Albuquerque, a name so exotic I had always longed to go there. *Could I get there alone?* I wondered.

Airlines were very helpful with wheelchairs at my destinations, allaying some of my concerns. And Mal, knowing that I was able to walk only a little way, met me in my wheelchair at the airport. I was soon comfortably settled in his huge four-wheel-drive car, driving slowly through the desert.

'I mustn't get booked for speeding,' he explained, 'because I have a gun in the car.' I laughed nervously, but it wasn't a joke. On the journey from Albuquerque to Rio Rancho, Mal kept pointing out suspicious-looking cars. 'They're drug dealers, for sure,' he whispered conspiratorially. I don't know how he knew.

Two huge guard dogs greeted us at the house, barking fiercely. I was beginning to think New Mexico was a dangerous place. Was I safe here alone with a man with a gun? Mal's wife was apparently delayed in Europe after a conference in Barcelona, about some military strategy, it seemed. She had lost her luggage, Mal said, and her homecoming would be delayed by twenty-four hours. He took me out to dinner that night and we exchanged small talk. The following day, somewhat to my relief, Cat returned home.

This couple, now retired, had been officers in the Iraq wars. Cat was a Major, in fact. She told me later she had been very angry when her husband enlisted in the Second Iraq War and after he was deployed she also re-engaged and was sent to Iraq too. I had never encountered any army people in my life so I was fascinated by the war stories Mal told me, and not a little scared, not least when he showed me all the guns he had at home. Following his lecture on safety while holding a gun, he gave me a Colt revolver, unloaded, to hold and it was surprisingly heavy.

A couple of days later we set off on a grand tour of the canyons. Army people, I learned, are super-efficient at organising and they looked after me with great kindness. I found Americans very sympathetic to disabled people and I was never made to feel a nuisance. Mal and Cat never once left me sitting alone, and always let me sit in the front seat of the car.

We stayed in motels and got up very early on the first day to view the amazing peaks in Bryce Canyon at dawn. The mileage was enormous, but my friends were indefatigable. We ended up at the 'Four Corners', the meeting point of four states – Utah, Colorado, Arizona and New Mexico. I bought the badge and had the photo taken to prove it. Of course there were climbs I could not do in a wheelchair, but always there were sights I could access and people were always willing to help.

After arriving back in Rio Rancho, Mal discovered there was a gun show on in town. This I had to see. It was a terrifying display, and as I sat in the car outside, a man passed me carrying the gun he had just purchased. 'Oh yes, it's all right,' Mal said. 'In this state you aren't allowed to carry concealed.'

There were no direct flights to London from Albuquerque, so after my seven days of travel and excitement I decided to stay overnight in Dallas and do some tacky tourist bits before returning home. First was visiting the set of *Dallas*. The ranch is preserved just as it was in the television series, but it is far out of town and I was able to visit only by a private tour. Expensive, but what the hell! The driver and guide played the *Dallas* theme tune on her radio as we turned into the familiar driveway and approached the house. I recognised the terrace where the Ewing family quarrelled, and the swimming pool, and yes, inside, there was J.R. Ewing Senior's portrait above the fireplace. The table was laid ready for dinner and the bathroom still sported the gold taps where Miss Ellie washed her hands. How much blood had flowed down that plug hole? I could visualise Bobby in the shower.

To continue my tour of the macabre, in the late afternoon my driver took me downtown to the Sixth Floor Museum, which was located in the former School Book Depository building and detailed the life, times and death of President J.F. Kennedy. I could pose outside for a photo with John and Jackie Kennedy on their final car ride superimposed in front of me. I was shown the green hillock where the second shot supposedly came from and finally I went up in the lift to the bookstore window where the scene for the assassination was set out.

That was my first experience of travelling alone to an unknown destination. I don't know if anyone else would have liked to share it with me, but I think it was the most exciting and terrifying journey of my life.

Gillian Gain is eighty-three years old and has been disabled for many years. She has always loved travelling and writing about her journeys. She lived in France with her husband, but after she was widowed she moved to a retirement flat in the UK.

When the Ice Melts
Suzy Pope

The table was covered with sheep's anklebones, polished smooth over hundreds of games of Shagai. With a delicate flick of my fingers, one white bone the size of my knuckle careered across the table and clattered to the floor. Lucas tutted. We'd been playing for two hours and I still didn't have the hang of it. I was frustrated and bored. I wasn't supposed to be in Mongolia anyway.

It had been Rachel's idea. She's the kind of friend who comes up with madcap adventures, throws country names around on a weekly basis and starts every plan with 'Why don't we just...'

'Let's do it,' she'd said, sloshing her pint. 'Two weeks, Beijing to Moscow via Mongolia. Mongolia, Suzy. I mean, why not?'

'OK, yeah. Let's do it.' I'd become caught up. 'I guess it's not too late to book for summer.'

'Screw summer. Everyone goes in summer. I want proper, Russian winter. That's how you're supposed to do Russia. Three weeks from now. I'm booking it tonight whether you're coming or not.'

I pictured us being the life of the group tour. Two laid-back young women with dazzling wit and a superior sense of spontaneity. I thought of the admiring looks on people's faces when we said, 'Oh, we just booked this a few weeks ago because we felt like it.'

I booked my flight to Beijing and called her.

'We're really doing this, aren't we?' I breathed into the phone.
Silence.

'Rachel?'

'Um, well, you see, the thing is, Mike's parents have this house in the Algarve, and he kind of wants me to go meet them. I mean, it's pretty much a free holiday, Suz. You should totally still go though.'

As I wandered the overcast streets of Beijing, brown slush soaked through my shoes. Cold seeped through my socks and deep into my bones. I could see why everybody went in summer.

Huddled into my jacket I trudged past towering skyscrapers. Every face was Chinese and it felt as though they were all staring at the Scottish girl walking in unsuitable footwear, alone in Beijing. Dinner was the worst. I took a notebook and pen with me and told myself: *For all they know, you are an important journalist. Nobody is looking at you and nobody is wondering why you are alone.*

I pointed at black-inked Mandarin words that looked more like hieroglyphics than a list of specials. When a dish of slimy animal insides appeared I would have given anything to have Rachel there to laugh with me. I ate in silence.

During the day I took pictures of myself smiling against the background of the Temple of Heaven or the Forbidden City.

'Beijing is the best,' I messaged Rachel, attaching a photo.

I couldn't wait to join the tour to Moscow. My mouth felt hot and stale from three days of not talking.

Small group tours are supposed to be a great way to meet like-minded travellers. They are also supposed to involve a group. Two people is not a group. Lucas barely said two words to me on the overnight train from Beijing to Ulan Bator. Stepping on to the platform we were hit with the raw cold of Mongolian winter.

'Chraast, man,' Lucas said in his thick South African accent. His long limbs were more suited to stretching out on a sweeping beach, not hunched and shivering in sixteen layers of wool. His frown looked as if it had been chiselled in ice – I'd never seen anyone look less like they wanted to be somewhere.

Click. One sheep's anklebone chinked against another. I lost another round of Shagai. Lucas leaned back, smug. The wood-burning stove hissed as a drip of melted snow fell from my woolly socks. It was our first day away from the cracked pavements, smoggy chimneys and block buildings of Ulan Bator. Outside the *ger* the sun shone over the ragged mountains and snow-swept plains of Gorkhi-Terelj National Park, but at minus-forty degrees my hair froze within minutes. My breath caught in my chest and my fingers became red and swollen. We were confined to our canvas room with nothing but a bag of sheep bones to keep us busy.

'Another round?' Lucas asked.

The fire died to embers and the tent walls shivered in the bitter wind. We hadn't eaten in hours and my stomach felt hollow. The clock ticked well past dinner time and, even though they had appeared at every Mongolian meal since we'd arrived, I would have given an organ for a plate of mutton dumplings. There were only two of us staying at the ger camp that week. What if the caretaker had forgotten all about us? Lucas's breath rose from his nostrils in spirals, like a dragon. I didn't fancy cuddling up to him for warmth.

I tapped out a text to Rachel: 'So pretty here. Mongolia is awesome. Trip of a *lifetime*.'

'Maybe it'll be warmer in the dinner tent,' I said.

Lucas shrugged.

A thousand tiny fingers pinched my cheeks and frost settled on my scarf as we waded through snow. Stars speckled the pitch-black sky, each one looking brighter and closer than I've ever seen. Around us was nothing but snow, sky and hills.

Entering the dinner tent, there was no smell of steaming mutton dumplings, no gust of warmth from the fire – just an empty kitchen and a tapestry Genghis Khan staring back at us.

'I wonder where the nearest Tesco is,' I joked.

Lucas didn't laugh. Maybe they didn't have Tesco in South Africa.

'Hello!' The caretaker's smiling face peered through the door flap. 'Tonight is New Year. We have *Tsagaan Sar* feast with my family.'

The word 'feast' conjured images of roasted wild carcasses, wine and a roaring fire.

'*Bayarlalaa*,' I said. Thank you.

Crammed into the caretaker's tent were his three daughters who cooked, his wife who tended the fires and our driver. The caretaker was dressed in purple silk robes that shimmered in the dull tent light. He wore a black pointed hat with a snaking pattern in gold. His family sat on beds around the circular walls, daughters tapping away on pink, breeze-block phones. The table was laid with deep-red dried meat and dried fruit. In the centre was a tower of sweet bread covered with sugar cubes and white pellets that looked like sticks of chalk.

'Bayarlalaa,' I said, stomach growling like a hungry snow leopard. Biting into a milky pellet, I nearly lost a tooth. The family's faces crinkled into smiles as they giggled in whispers to each other. The driver hissed to get my attention and made a sucking noise. The pellet tasted like sour yoghurt.

The caretaker announced something in Mongolian and removed the lid from a boiling pot on the stove. Saliva pooled in my mouth as I braced myself to be hit with the smell of slow-cooked meat. It never came. Instead the caretaker ladled milk tea into ornate bowls. I accepted a bowl with my right hand, and let the weirdly salty liquid send warmth to my bones.

I chewed a bit of dried yak meat, trying to trick my stomach into thinking it was being fed. The caretaker produced two large bottles of vodka. Genghis Khan's stern face on the label mirrored Lucas's expression. We accepted shots with our right hand, like the driver had told us, and the clear liquid burned the pit of my empty stomach.

As the pleasant hum of alcohol warmed my limbs, the caretaker stood up and the tent fell silent. He started to sing in whispery Mongolian, a tear creeping to the corner of his eye as he placed a hand on his heart.

'Mongolian national anthem,' the driver said. Even the youngest, sulking teenage daughter stopped looking at her phone and listened. I looked over at Lucas. His mouth was a tight line, but the corners of his eyes had softened.

The caretaker gestured to me. Panic rose in my chest. My best singing voice sounds like a chorus of yaks in labour. If Rachel were here we could shriek our way through ironic covers of the Spice Girls' greatest hits. Alone, everything was ten times more daunting.

I waved my arms in the universal sign for 'No, no, I couldn't possibly,' but was pulled to my feet anyway. I cleared my throat to start the song that had been cycling through my head since we'd arrived in Mongolia.

'I really can't stay...' I started.

Lucas got to his feet.

'Baby it's cold outside,' he replied in a perfect tenor.

By the time we reached the chorus, Lucas's frozen brow had melted completely into a relaxed, lazy smile. The crowd went wild.

We bowed and the smell of cooked meat filled the tent as a daughter carried in a tray tottering with slippery mutton dumplings. I accepted a plate piled high as though it were a Grammy, repeating 'Bayarlalaa' over and over to the warm, happy faces around me.

We spent the rest of the night filling hollow stomachs with dumplings and listening to the caretaker and his family lilt through ancient folk songs. The driver gave us a song sung right in the back of his throat. Lucas and I lurched through 'Hey Jude', making everyone join in with the 'na-na-na-nana-na-nas'.

During the five solid days on the train to Moscow I forgot about the surly man that had stepped off the train in Ulan Bator. Lucas and I spun a web of in-jokes and whisked up an instant friendship.

Back in Scotland, when I met Rachel for coffee, I showed off pictures of Lucas and me in front of St Basil's Cathedral, like two figures in a snow globe.

'We should totally take the train through Vietnam next year,' Rachel said.

'Sure,' I replied. I'd become rather fond of long train journeys. If Rachel flaked out on me I could always see if Lucas was up for it.

Suzy Pope likes the boring parts of travel best. Timetables, waiting rooms, long train journeys, planning and research. After winning various travel-writing competitions, she has been published in magazines such as *Geographical*, *National Geographic Traveller* and *Wanderlust*.

Mollie

Hilary Bradt

I didn't want to travel alone. I don't like travelling alone. But travelling with a companion who so obviously hated me was worse than travelling alone. And Mollie hated me.

Mollie was a Connemara pony, the essential component for achieving a childhood dream: a leisurely long-distance ride through ever-changing scenery. I decided that Ireland fitted the bill perfectly.

It had taken me four years to prepare for the trip. It was a long-held ambition but also, more subtly, an 'I can do this' act of defiance after having spent ten happy years travelling with my husband. To my acquaintances I was the same intrepid woman they knew, or thought they knew – always up for an adventure, fearless in the face of danger, bouncing back after the trauma of divorce. What most of them didn't know is that from my earliest years I've been shy. An introvert. With maturity I learned to assume a mask of self-confidence and chattiness, but it never came naturally and this was my Achilles Heel as a traveller.

When I was married to George it was easy. He had no social fears and, in his company, nor had I. Now I was alone I wanted to learn to *like* being alone, and that was proving to be a slow process. Physical dangers were no problem; they're part and parcel of adventurous travel, and there's something almost refreshing about rational fear.

It's irrational fear that's so debilitating because of the feeling of foolishness that goes with it. It's hard to admit that someone who has survived detention in Uganda and Ethiopia with her nerves intact, quakes at the thought of making a phone call, entering a crowded room or ringing a doorbell.

As well as my conscious worries about the trip, a variety of subconscious ones surfaced in a rich crop of dreams. Many of them had elements of realism, as the one where I had just bought a horse and had pitched my tent in a busy campsite. The field was full of tents, spaced as neatly and regularly as war cemetery crosses. Through this order my disorderly horse wandered, crawling into other people's tents and making a thorough nuisance of itself. I decided I must tether it. It was only after I bent down to attach the strap to its leg that I realised, to my horror, that I hadn't inspected all of the horse when I bought it. It was a fine-looking animal – from the body up – but its legs were as tiny and slender as a sheep's. No way could it carry me and the luggage.

Luggage. That had been my preoccupation for at least a year. I'd bought lightweight and waterproof clothing and gear for myself, but equipping a horse for a journey of several months was something new. I bought saddlebags, a nosebag and a hobble from America, a head collar in Peru and a sheepskin in Ecuador. A neighbour provided the perfect saddle. With this assembly of the best the international horse world would provide I was all set. Consciously, anyway. In one dream I was all saddled up and ready to go when the horse turned round and said sharply, 'Don't you think you can do better than that?' I saw its point; instead of a saddle there was my blue kitchen chair on its back.

It was only when I stood on the platform of Beaconsfield Station that the realisation dawned that one person can't, physically, carry five bags from Buckinghamshire to the west of Ireland. Another drawback of travelling alone. There would be no-one to watch the luggage while the other went off to investigate – not that I should dignify those bursting bin-liners by calling them luggage. The sheer awfulness of getting them to Dublin and then to Galway pushed all other worries from my mind. For the first stretch I booked a coach direct from London to Dublin, assuming that the coach went on to the ferry. Not so. It dropped us on the dock at Holyhead, seemingly miles from the boat, and we were told to remove all our luggage. Another coach would meet us on the other side, so they said. I managed to find a trolley lurking in some dark recess and was just piling everything on when an officious man appeared and said, 'You're doing it all wrong.' He took all my things off and loaded the trolley with cases belonging to a girl standing next to me. Then came my plastic bags. The girl was most grateful and I was not particularly gracious as I pushed the thing towards the mass of people waiting to board the boat. Then, of course, I wasn't allowed to take the trolley on board so I had to heave my stuff on in relays, banging the backs of people's knees as I went. Some turned round to remonstrate but, after a look at my furious face, changed their minds. I just left it all in a pile near the gangway.

Arrival at Dún Laoghaire, Dublin's port, was no easier. The new coach had no luggage compartment. I struggled inside with my five bags, clunking people on the head with the saddle which was starting to emerge from its torn plastic bag, and swearing instead of apologising. This procedure was repeated, with variations, until I got to Galway. At least there was no time to get anxious about the next stage: buying a horse.

I had a list of telephone numbers and stood in a phone box steeling myself to call these possible horse dealers one by one. My biggest dread, phoning strangers, was made even more frightening by the fact that they all seemed to be Irish aristocracy. None admitted to having ponies for sale, but told me with confidence that I should contact Willy Leahy, a horse dealer and owner of the region's trekking stable. And, yes, he had several suitable ponies and, as an added bonus, if I found one I liked I could join his first trek of the season for free. That last comment sealed the deal. The enormity of what I was about to embark on was giving me sleepless nights, and the opportunity to get to know my new pony, coax my riding muscles into shape and learn how to deal with the rocky, boggy terrain of County Galway was an opportunity not to be missed.

So it was that I bought Mollie, a sturdy white Connemara pony with dapple grey flanks and a flowing mane and tail. Mollie had spent the winter, as always, roaming the hills of Connemara with her herd before being rounded for the summer trekking season. She knew the routine: have fun with her companions treading familiar paths and indulge in some sea bathing. She was my dream pony and I was prepared to love her unconditionally. She, however, saw no reason to return the compliment when forced to leave her equine friends and travel solo.

Our response to the first night spent without our recent companions was similar. Hers was unmitigated horror. She was tethered for the first time in her life in the grounds of the posh hotel where I had enjoyed a boozy farewell meal with the group, and I was in my tent unable to sleep because of my need to get up at intervals to untangle the tether and offer her words of comfort. That first day the hills of Galway echoed with her neighs as she tried to locate her friends, and I wondered gloomily what I had got myself into. It was clear that Mollie was even less enthusiastic about solo travel than I was.

The next night was very much better for both of us. Invited to share a meal and a cosy fireside with a hospitable farming family, I pitched my tent in their orchard and turned Mollie loose into a spacious field to catch up with her own eating. After such a pleasant night, the next day should have been a doddle. But Mollie was equally appreciative of the farmer's hospitality and had no intention of relinquishing it. 'Come on Mollie, good girl!' I said with gentle horse-loving tones and equicide in my heart as I trudged after her through long, dew-soaked grass. I had left her head collar on just in case, but Mollie, grazing nonchalantly, kept an ear cocked for my soothing pleasantries and a sneer on her lips, until I was a few feet away, then took off at a brisk trot.

After half an hour I realised she was not going to warm to me and I'd have to resort to bribery. The family was out, but fortunately I had spotted a sack of horse nuts outside the kitchen door. Filling a bucket with these treats I went back to the field. Mollie let me get a little closer and showed interest, but however stealthily I reached out my hand, she always saw it coming and trotted off. However, my arrival with a bucket hadn't gone unnoticed by the herd of bullocks in the neighbouring field and they galloped up and down the fence bellowing encouragement whenever I seemed to be approaching them.

Eventually Mollie's greed got the better of her and I managed to take hold of her head collar. Once caught, she accepted the situation with equanimity and I was able to clip on the lead rein and start for the gate. Here I was confronted with a new problem: two gates were secured with one bit of rope, and if I opened the gate to Mollie's field, the one giving the bullocks access to the road swung open. They were clustered there excitedly waiting for me to deliver the goodies in the bucket. I had to tie Mollie to the gate-post while I unfastened the rope securing the two gates, propping them shut while I climbed back over the stone wall into Mollie's field. The top boulders gave way. I fell heavily with a squawk of pain. Mollie took fright, pulled back and broke her lead rein; the gate swung open and three bullocks escaped into the road. I was close to tears. My attempts to drive the bullocks back into the field only resulted in the escape of two more. I had a bruised arm, a gashed ankle; Mollie was once again enjoying her freedom and I'd committed the cardinal sin of damaging a fence and letting out livestock. I was not having a good time.

Of course, things got better. As the weeks passed I found that I loved being alone. The days were filled with sunshine (yes, in Ireland!) and spring flowers, views of mountains and tiny fields carved out of the stony landscape, and rounded by nights in my little tent, lulled by Mollie's rhythmic munching. Mollie accepted her fate and became almost obliging, although she had a habit of looking at me in surprise, as if to say, 'Goodness, are you still here?' before shutting her eyes and turning her head away. She also sighed a lot. Then, one morning a couple of weeks into our trek, I went to collect her from the farmer's field and she walked towards me, giving a small whicker. Just the merest flutter of her nostrils, but it was enough.

We were going to get on just fine.

Hilary Bradt never grew out of her childhood horsiness, much to the despair of the adults around her, though she did take a rather long break from riding after founding Bradt Travel Guides in 1974. She got back in the saddle ten years later to ride a thousand miles through the west of Ireland, a journey described in her two books, *Connemara Mollie* and *Dingle Peggy*, both published by Bradt.

Tips

With no companion to watch your bag... time your toilet break *before* you collect your bag from the carousel at the airport, or beeline for the disabled toilet for some extra room if you do have to haul it in with you. If you need to leave your bag unattended on a train or bus, do so just after a stop to give yourself time to report a theft if it does happen. Wedging your bag into an awkward position on a luggage rack can also deter people from trying to steal it.

To take photos of yourself... If you don't do selfies, you'll have to hand your camera to someone else to take your picture – a worrying prospect if you're travelling with an expensive one. Find someone with a better camera than your own to take the snap for you – chances are they won't want to steal your inferior model, and they'll probably know how to frame a decent shot too.

It's not uncommon for solo travellers (women in particular) to be targeted for scams, as people can assume that you're vulnerable. Carry yourself with conviction – strong and confident body language can go a long way. Be charming and polite at first, smiling to try and diffuse the situation, but if problems continue, walk away and find what you need elsewhere. If it's a situation that you can't walk away from, such as being charged fake fees, firmly stand your ground and kick up a fuss. You might even have to really overreact, but sometimes it's the only way to avoid being ripped off.

Getting sick while abroad alone can be very miserable. It's better to let someone else know that you're not feeling well – a member of staff at your hotel, for example. It's reassuring to know that someone else has their eye on you, and you'd be surprised by how many people are eager to help a traveller in need.

Wanderlust **magazine** www.wanderlust.co.uk

Carry or do something unlikely – it's a conversation starter! One time, I bought a beautiful old kettle while in Peru before thinking how I would get it in my bag. People laughed to see me travelling with a rusty kettle as a companion. Another time I was making a handmade patchwork quilt and used travelling time to sew the pieces together. I could never have imagined how many people thought this was a great ice-breaker and I spent nearly every plane, train, bus and boat journey meeting fellow passengers. *Claire Morsman*

What Am I Doing Here?

This is surely the question frequently asked by the lone traveller as extraordinary events unfold, whether it's coming to terms with being alone in a mountain retreat with no electricity, battling a Shetland gale, or wondering how you ended up in a Beijing hotel room still, apparently, occupied by another guest. Claire Morsman reflects how wrong first impressions can be: 'Now I realised my early apprehension had been fuelled by a fear of joining in', Dom Tulett finds that homesickness may be just part of travel, and Ella Pawlik immerses herself in Sulawesi, with the knowledge that 'there are beautiful things happening all the time, we just need to look for them'.

Cycling Shetland
Pat Smith

The ferry from Mainland to the isle of Yell thudded and thumped through the strait then juddered as a larger-than-usual wave smashed against the passenger lounge window. I staggered then regained my balance in the cold, draughty and functional room.

Ignoring the interested gaze of other passengers I perched on an almost-padded grey chair, pulled off my damp boots, soggy socks and waterproof trousers then excavated cycle pannier bag number two.

Yes, no, yes!

I pulled out my one pair of waterproof socks and almost kissed them before threading them on to my numb feet which had turned red with cold.

It was March and I was cycling my way to the northernmost point of Shetland. I had already fought wind which drove horizontal arrows of rain into my face as I pedalled slowly up long, steady hills which sapped my energy and left me gasping for breath.

I needed all the help I could get.

Waterproof socks? Oh, for bionic legs, a turbo-charged engine and Superman to push me up hills.

Superman…

How I needed my very own Superman, but at this very moment he was spread out on his comfy sofa, warm and well fed, but plastered.

Not with alcohol but plaster of Paris.

Exactly two days and seventeen minutes before he was to join me for the assault on Shetland my mobile phone rang.

'Pat, I'm in casualty. Broken leg.'

'Whaaat?'

Selfish thoughts massacred compassion.

'You won't be joining me? Oh, and… errr sorry… it must hurt a lot.'

He told me his sad tale, but I only half listened as an acid avalanche hit my stomach.

Who would sort out the satnav, tell stupid jokes to keep me going and hold my bike when I wanted to pee? What if I had a *puncture*?

I'd just have to cope, though I feared the days would be grey without him.

The ferry grated against concrete.

We'd arrived.

Three cars drove off the ramp and disappeared up the hill before I'd wheeled my bike off the ferry. Three more cars and a van boarded the boat as if all the devils from hell were after them.

I stood alone and watched the red-funnelled ferry as it bucked away from me across the white-capped, streaming grey waves and back to Mainland.

The port didn't have a name, just a desolate car park, one tiny waiting room and a red double-decker bus left in a corner out of the wind with 'CAFE' writ large across the front. Closed, of course. With not a house or car in sight. The island of Yell has around a thousand inhabitants and clearly none of them lived anywhere near.

I was on my own.

I knew with cold certainty that once I climbed the slope out of the port the wind would catch me in its teeth then rattle and shake me without mercy.

And it did.

It buffeted me sideways and frontwards as I set off along the single-track B road, heading north. Less than twenty miles away was Gutcher, my bed-and-breakfast destination.

Shards of ice-cold rain spat at my face and runnels of water drenched my back as I pedalled through miles of empty moorland. Telegraph posts lined the road like blackened signposts to my doom and scraps of bin liners skewered against barbed-wire fences streamed in the wind like monstrous, deformed bats.

Nothing else moved. Only me. For hours.

I cycled up long, relentless slopes into the vicious wind. I even had to pedal downhill – how unfair. To me, cycling was a metaphor for life – uphill was the hard part but the glorious downhill glide followed like sunshine after rain. Clearly this was not the case in Shetland.

But I was a woman with a mission. At sixty-seven, virtuous pensioner and member of the University of the Third Age, with knees, hips and eyesight almost intact, I had decided to cycle a very slow six thousand miles around the United Kingdom, laden with four pannier bags and around twenty kilograms of luggage.

A few friends might join me en route. That's if they didn't break legs, arms or anything else important.

I planned to head south to the Isles of Scilly, west to the Dingle Peninsula of southern Ireland, east to Lowestoft Ness and to the furthest point north of the furthest-inhabited British island. This was the Hermaness National Nature Reserve on the island of Unst in Shetland.

These islands are isolated. Their nearest railway station is in Norway and it's further from Shetland to Edinburgh than from Edinburgh to London.

It was time to stop, rub some sensation into my hands, feel miserably lonely and eat chocolate. I crouched in the shelter of a derelict croft, its roof timbers collapsed inside sagging stone walls. Perhaps the inhabitants had experienced one too many uphills. Life in Shetland is tough, though easier than it once was. Before roads, people travelled by boat from one coastal hamlet to the next. To encourage people to use cars, for many years non-Mainlanders were allowed to drive without passing a test, as long as their vehicles displayed L plates.

Shetland has few roads, but this has its compensations. I'd learned one thing about myself as a traveller – I would get lost. Daily. Even with a satnav to help. It once directed me to a Church Road about ten miles away from the one I wanted and I had to camp in a field. When I meet a canal, it's three to one that I'll head the wrong way. So it was refreshing to realise that on Shetland there were no wrong turnings because there were no turnings.

As if on cue, my road curved downhill – at last out of the wind – to a sheltered village close to the sea.

Mid Yell.

The road took me close to a small, stony beach with black rocks stretching long arms into the sea and a short pier standing sturdy against the waves.

The area was first inhabited by Vikings in the ninth century and it's easy to see why; it made a perfect port for small boats, protected as it was from wind and waves.

Most of the islanders live there, in well-kept grey or whitewashed bungalows and houses. It has a church, leisure centre, medical facilities and school.

And a shop. A shop...

I dismounted and walked stiffly towards a derelict stone building with blank, grey-eyed windows covered with corrugated iron. Next to it sheltered a long, low cabin with lights round the windows and posters on the door. What shopkeepers in such an isolated spot would waste their time opening on a Sunday? Anyway it would probably stock only out-of-date newspapers, stale bread and soggy apples.

I realised how wrong I was the moment I pushed open the door. A blast of semi-tropical air hit my face and almost blinded me. Once I'd wiped the fog from my specs I saw that Links House Store was the place to be on a stormy Sunday afternoon.

Eight teenagers wrapped in weatherproofs lounged around the coffee machine; three older women in formal Sunday dresses and coats stood chatting by the counter and a couple with a lollipop-sucking toddler in a buggy managed to block the aisle. People smiled at me, tactfully ignoring the growing puddle that my waterproofs left as I tried to persuade the coffee machine to give me hot chocolate.

A young dark-haired man wearing a hand-knitted pullover took the coins out of my numb hand, pressed the correct buttons and presented me with the drink that I yearned for, as a girl stood up to let me have the single chair.

Inside was warm, bright and friendly with that slight steaminess of people with damp clothes and the gentle curiosity of those who feel they are encountering insanity.

Rain beat against the windows; through them I saw wind-whipped grey waves racing across the bay. I stalled, finding things to do to avoid that dreadful moment when I would leave and face the cold blasts of a March wind.

I went to the toilet, spent ages washing my hands, checked my purse, bought some biscuits, then decided to phone my hosts who lived in the remote Old Post Office at Gutcher.

They were expecting me to arrive by early afternoon and I was late.

'Only seven miles to go,' they told me.

'Two hours?' I said hopefully.

I tried to pedal fast. Impossible. The rain had stopped, but the wind banged against me and there was another long, slow hill to creep up. Was I managing three miles per hour? Or less? With dripping nose, watery eyes, numb hands – and did I still have feet? – I must have looked a pathetic figure as I heaved myself onwards. Oh, how I needed someone to tell me something funny to encourage me – best of all, someone to cycle in front of me so I could use them as a windbreak.

But it's strange – just when you think you can't take any more, calm invades body and mind.

It can't get any worse, you think, and strangely it doesn't.

Though cold, drenched and numb I refused to be miserable. *I will not let the weather ruin this experience*, I thought as I struggled on.

An abandoned croft beckoned. Set in the lee of the hill its heaped and grimy stone walls offered shelter and a chance to rest.

A blanket of silence wrapped itself round me.

I could hear nothing. Nothing at all.

I gazed at rolling moorland with faded shades of brown and orange flowing and blending into each other. Tussocky, uneven grasslands were speckled with rocks and grey-white sheep faced away from the wind as they munched. A few tiny, isolated bungalows crouched in the heather like intruders in the vastness.

White clouds scudded across the sky, startling against the looming dark grey which signalled more rain to come as gulls soared and leapt the currents, riding the wind as Viking invaders had once ridden the waves.

Our ancestors had learnt to live with land and sea, accepting whatever it offered them, noting every stone or rock, watching each movement of cloud and wave, anticipating and coping with rain and storms as they searched for a safe harbour, for their lives depended on this awareness.

This wasn't the countryside that you see through the misted windows of an overwarm car – no, this was fresh, pure and real, with a wild beauty that soared into my mind.

I took deep breaths of untainted air and rejoiced.

At the same time I knew I needed to be alone right now, alone to look where I wanted, think what I needed and let myself merge with the experience. To have shared my vision of this harsh landscape with anyone at all would have changed everything.

At that moment I was the only person in the universe.

And that was right.

I was pushing my bike up yet another hill when a car appeared in front of me then stopped.

'Pat?' the driver said. 'I'm Peter, from the Post Office. We were a bit worried, especially as it's getting dark. Would you like to pop your bike into the car?'

I was about to fall at his feet in worship, then paused. The road would soon turn away from the wind. It would be downhill.

'Could you possibly take my pannier bags? And have a pot of tea ready?' I asked.

Without the extra twenty kilograms my bike turned from carthorse to racehorse.

I zoomed along, backed by the wind, then almost floated down the hill towards a long, grey stone building with a red telephone box outside. I'd arrived.

'How was the journey?' asked Anne, Peter's wife, thirty minutes later.

I bit into my slice of homemade fruitcake and snuggled my toes into the rug.

Showered and changed, warm and comfortable, I could laugh.

'It wasn't easy, but I did it. Somehow.'

I'd struggled against everything wind, rain and landscape could throw against me. I'd had to face it on my own and I was exhausted.

But the experience had been more precious than gold dust. I'd seen things and thought things that would stay with me forever.

Born in Gibraltar in 1949, **Pat Smith** was shipped back to England in a wooden drawer when four months old. At the age of seven she flew to Singapore, which took five days but that didn't diminish her joy. Since then she has lived in Singapore, Hong Kong, Serbia and Ethiopia. She earned her keep as a teacher but took a gap year when fifty-two and travelled from Dover to Cape Town by truck. She celebrated retirement by backpacking solo around the world, and in 2016 cycled around Britain.

The Mountain Retreat

Martha Hales

I found myself stomping up the cold stone steps of a friend's mountain bolthole almost by accident. A few misplaced 'oohs' and 'aahs' over photos of the newly acquired chalet; some mild enthusiasm when I was invited to use it, and somehow the path of least resistance had led me here, keys and instructions in hand. 'Think of it as a gift,' she had said.

1. Collect torch from mailbox. *OK, managed that.*
2. Larger key unlocks front door. *Right, I'm in.*
3. Use torch to locate fuse box inside on right-hand side of door frame. *Got it.*
4. Push largest black switch up for power. *Done.*
5. Light switch to left of door frame.

Click. *Oh.* Click click click. *Hmmm. Duff bulb? Find another light switch.* Click click click. No light. *Try fuse box again.*

All possible combinations of switches on, off, up and down exhausted, I fought my way through creaky shutters out on to the balcony and flopped into a seat, wiping cobwebs from my brow and trying not to cry. Nothing like a thorny issue involving cables or pipes to remind me of how alone I was, up a mountain in Italy, with no idea what to do next. I let one quiet sob escape, but forced the rest back. If I wasn't careful the floodgates would open. I had let myself be talked into this trip with words like 'peaceful' and 'retreat', but so far it was anything but.

How could it have gone so wrong already? I'd only got as far as instruction number five. I checked the list. Five out of sixty-eight. I glanced through pages of helpful tips on bus times and local eateries, stopcocks and firewood, but there was nothing about how to solve a lack of power.

Two thoughts – *middle of nowhere* and *don't speak the language* – suddenly crystallised in my mind. My heart began to race. Why had I agreed to this trip anyway? I felt almost as if I had arrived through the sheer force of my friend K's determination to get me here after my 'tough year'. I took some deep breaths, and poured out my woes to a passing lizard. I felt lonely and helpless as afternoon began sliding into evening. I decided the power problem would have to wait. I didn't have rational thought on my side at that moment.

A rootle around the chalet turned up wine, water, nuts and candles. Along with the torch I figured that would tide me over until the next day when I could address the problem with renewed vigour. A couple of glasses of red and a slow examination of the view fading in the dusk proved restorative, yet the sweep of green from a valley of villages and vines to the glitter of blue lake seemed only to mock me in my solitude. A view as glorious as this one deserved to be shared. Once the pink glow had receded from the snowy peaks opposite, I turned in for the night.

My breath formed puffy clouds above the duvet when I woke up first thing. An altitude of 750 metres in early spring will do that. It didn't take long to discover that the shower, cooker, hot water boiler and kettle all ran on electricity. So I was un-showered, un-coffeed and cold when I approached the uncooperative fuse box. I tried good cop, bad cop and downright blasphemous cop, but no amount of cajoling, swearing or manic clicking of switches would restore the current, so I set out to find someone who knew what to do. A few of the elderly ladies of the village stood gossiping by the church. I envied them their camaraderie.

'NO POWER,' I said, too loudly, slashing my hand across my throat in an attempt to communicate the problem to the handful of men propping up the village bar. I got a couple of shrugs and a few pairs of eyes narrowed in confusion. I repeated the throat slashing motion and pointed at the light switch.

'Electricity. No. Zero.' I vigorously shook my head. The men still looked nonplussed. I let out a big sigh. So far this was not quite the calming 'gift' of a mountain retreat I had hoped for. And I really didn't want to admit to K that I had failed to fix the first problem that cropped up on my first solo holiday.

Scraping stools and downing thimblefuls of wine, two of the patrons of the bar got up and hurled a string of Italian at me. I looked as helpless as I could and gestured towards the door. But even when they had gathered quite a few similarly practical types to investigate, much fruitless clicking of switches and muttering didn't advance the situation. Several upturned palms showed me they couldn't fix the problem. As they left they trailed silence in their wake.

As the sun wheeled higher in the sky and the day began to warm up, the lack of electricity seemed less important. A directionless stroll through the steep cobbled lanes of the village revealed glimpses of the distant lake between the rooftops. The hay-scented mountain air felt cleansing and vital as I followed a switchback track among the meadows until I was high above the rooflines. I had to admit, K had picked her bolthole well. The view was divine. A cluster of stone houses straggled up the backbone of the hill, with a jaunty bell tower at the foot of the village and grassy slopes all around. Muffled goat bells chimed in the hollows of the valley, while green peaks loomed above. A road meandered, stitching farms and hamlets together on its way down the hill through the pastures to the lake.

Back at K's chalet I dug out a tin of cannellini beans. Even with some good oil and fresh sage plucked from a bush by the door they reminded me that I was facing the prospect of seven days with no warm food or drink, no showers and no light. Time to send K a text.

'No electricity supply. Have tried everything I can think of. Neighbours can't work out why either. Any ideas? Apart from that, all lovely! Great spot. x'

An hour turned into an afternoon, and then into another day, but K didn't reply. I gave up trying to get the power on and thought round the problem, using an old pan over the fire for heating coffee and food, and lighting candles at dusk. My days passed in a pastoral daze, wandering among the vines and orchards on the south-facing slopes or puffing up cobbled mule tracks to mountain trattorias. The lakes and mountains of Lombardy were serene in the sunlight and sparklingly clear air. Blue bonfire smoke hung in distant valleys and buzzards spiralled above. The 'tough year' was receding a little from my thoughts and, best of all, I began to enjoy the solitude.

Some days later, having discounted reconnection entirely, I was amazed at how easy it became to survive off-grid once the mental adjustment had been made, quickly settling into a morning routine of replenishing stocks of candles, firewood, wine and wet wipes. How little I cared that nobody arrived to ease my plight. I immersed myself in books and relished the lack of interruptions. The battery died on my phone, I had to fill the bed with hot-water bottles before diving in, and I washed in a bucket in front of the fire. It felt like quite an adventure, if a rather chilly and unhygienic one.

Stinking of wood smoke and mild neglect is pretty much *de rigueur* up at that altitude, for in the stone hamlets which dot the mountains above Lake Como's northern shores the simple life prevails. Clothes are washed at the *fontana*, milk comes daily from a cow, and goat herding is an aspirational career choice. My unwashed hair was hardly breaking news. It was liberating to realise that no-one was likely to notice my less-than-polished appearance.

The bubble burst when I reached Malpensa Airport in Milan. In the queue for security among the immaculate Italians with their buckled and bowed children and coordinating designer luggage, I was suddenly acutely aware that my unkempt chic did not cut the Milanese mustard. My standards fell far short, but no matter. I boarded the plane with head held high. Despite my dishevelled air I was proud of myself. A week in the mountains without power or company. I had survived.

Martha Hales might like words even more than people. Having spent twelve years exploring Europe and the Middle East, turning her hand to tour guiding, ski rep-ing,  cheese eating and wine tasting along the way, she now devotes much of her time to words. When she isn't writing, she's probably eating cheese.

Solo Ways in Sulawesi
Ella Pawlik

Just before I leave, I read that there are around half a million people in the sky at any one time. The flight out of soggy Heathrow is surreal. An emotional kaleidoscope hurtling through the troposphere, I'm one in half a million, wishing that 'I' were 'we', and we were two in half a million. At 6.30 a.m. English time we land in Singapore. I head straight outside to the Cactus Garden without passing Go, and sit in a sky-tantrum storm with probably the best pint of my life (and I'm not afraid to admit there have been a few). While I'm there I watch a fat line of fat tropical ants dodging fat raindrops and making their fat way across the floor. While staring at them, I realise that going away was definitely the right decision, even if I am flying solo.

During the onward night flight – now local time – to Jakarta I get bored and pull up the window shutter. The sea is a deep, royal purple and a silvery-bright strip of moonlight fractures it in two. Sometimes a little desert island pops up to say hello, waving its palm tree hands at the sky. This scene makes me remember that there are beautiful things happening all the time – we just need to look for them. Then the air hostess tells me to pull the shutter down and this makes me remember that rules are happening all the time, and we just need to try and ignore them.

After more stops, and starts, and stops again, I finally, eventually, land in sultry Makassar and am immediately cornered by the oppressive heat, and by a guy called Ahmed who asks me where my boyfriend is. I tell him my boyfriend is waiting for me at the hostel. My mythical man is, fortuitously, a more proficient traveller than I am, and will always be one step ahead. Lovely chap. Awfully quiet though.

People smile and shout, 'Mister! Mister! English! Manchester!' at me as I, laden with sweat and an element of confusion, explore the city. Manchester because of football, presumably. And Mister because that's just what they seem to say to foreigners (I try not to take it personally), although I don't see many other Mister Manchesters here. Maybe I'm staying in the wrong part of town. Without anyone else to confer with, I base my decisions on the sturdy foundations of guesswork and blind hope. I vex myself about relying on the fact that people will speak English to me (it's arrogant, but I have no other choice), and try to learn some Indonesian. I get the basics – a few numbers, some polite phrases and questions – down, but beyond that I rely on wild gesticulations to get my points across. This is reminiscent of when I was on Tioman Island and the people who lived there told me I reminded them of Mr Bean. So that's nice.

I head out of Makassar quick smart to Pantai Bira, a little village with a large number of goats. At the weekend there are quite a few holidaying locals who all want to take photos of me and shake my hand. It feels a little bit like being a celebrity, except I haven't done anything commendable. Oh. Hang on, so it's exactly like being a celebrity. I take photos of the goats and the locals take photos of me. Sometimes I wish that one of the goats would pick up a camera and take pictures of the locals, and then we'd all be in a satisfyingly weird snapshot circle. This never happens. There's no wireless in Bira and no internet kiosks. I feel naked, but then learn to enjoy it, realising I could well be a technological nudist at heart. I am on my own and I am free.

Dive. Breathe in. Breathe out. I see blacktip reef sharks, nudibranchs, bumphead parrotfish (Woi, fatties!), batfish, squirrelfish, moray eels, giant clams, gargantuan gorgonian fans, more brain coral than I can think about and lots of other weird and wonderfuls. Beautiful things really are everywhere, and I really go down into the blue to look for them. Bad things are also everywhere though, and some parts of Bira I really don't like. The main beach is littered with litter and the dive school drops anchor on coral instead of using buoys. I get uppity and down, but I can't tell anyone because my Mr Bean moves don't extend that far.

A self-made concern that becomes increasingly prevalent is how dire my sense of direction is. Even with a map, I set off in the wrong direction. Every. Single. Time. How this is possible I don't know. I always get there in the end; it just takes a while and is usually done by process of elimination rather than efficacy. I'm a classic traveller cliché – I'm (getting lost and then) finding myself.

Buses help. The drivers have more confidence about where they're going, and I'm happy to sit back and watch the busy, unfamiliar faces and brightly coloured buildings flash by. I head north. Back to Makassar. Then to Tana Toraja. And onwards. Upwards. Towards the Togean Islands. Not long into a nineteen-hour bus journey I realise I'm in an absolute textbook bus-on-mountain-precipice-in-the-rainy-season scenario. We drive higher and the clouds block the view below until I'm lulled into a false sense of security that if the bus falls off I'll land on a soft white cushion, possibly with a Care Bear or two to hold my hands. The longest part of the journey is waiting at 'the crossing', an area of the road that has eroded into a sandpit. We join a long, beeping queue of heavy vehicles and wait our turn to not go and play in the sand. When we finally cross it the bus skids and we come out the other side at a funny angle and teeter on the edge of the mountainside, passengers' knuckles communally white, before heading off on our merry way again. I haven't spoken a word the whole time.

A quick stop-off in Tentena, a swim in the glorious lake, and out on another bus, past stalls of fried bats and goldfish and the sound of explosions. It's December, so Christmas celebrations have started. And that means boys spend the entire month throwing firecrackers called 'atom bombs' on to the ground when you walk past. Because, you know, nothing says 'I love you, Jesus' like perforating your neighbour's eardrums.

I make best friends with an old lady on the bus who is about the size of one of my fingers. We can't say anything to each other, but she keeps resting her hand on my arm and giving me illuminating smiles, each tooth a dangling white lantern. The second part of the journey is in a Toyota Kijang driven by central Sulawesi rude boys who listen to Indo Trance and won't make eye contact with me. I feel a bit vulnerable (no-one knows where I am, I don't have a phone and even if I did, who would I call anyway?), but I finally arrive in Ampana. The last dry land before the Togeans.

As is the way when you're on your own, I meet all sorts while I'm waiting a few days for the boat. Sometimes 'the meantime' – the bits in between the actual things – ends up being the most interesting. There's some sort of conference at the place I'm staying. All the attendees arrive in advance, and I spend a surreal evening chatting to official-looking men from Palu. One man features more prominently than most as he's in the room next to me. He's from Jakarta and wants to tell me all about his seaweed business. He's obviously learnt enough English to explain his work, but beyond that his vocabulary is understandably limited. We talk about seaweed, and seaweed only.

I actually really make it to the Togeans the next day. They are definitely *a thing*. Quite possibly *the thing* to end all things. Perhaps I was just trying to make myself feel better with all that meantime nonsense.

After days of loud engines and silent thoughts escaping through dirt filters on bus windows, I step off the boat into a sweltering, sandy paradise. The sea is over thirty degrees and the air is so hot it feels like I'm standing in front of a hairdryer. It's like being given a constant spa treatment, except I look awful. The view from my hut is so lovely I feel as though I'm on honeymoon with myself. Someone is definitely missing – I check under the double bed, but only find a dead hermit crab and confirmation of solitude. So I pull myself together, tell myself I look beautiful and hold hands with myself as I walk down the jetty to have a romantic sunset beer on my own.

Life is deliciously simple on this island of the Togeans. No shops, restaurants or anythings. No roads. The only sounds are cicadas, geckos and a very loud kingfisher. I meet some other travellers and we go snorkelling in a saltwater lake full of jellyfish which, despite the fact that I know they're special ones that don't sting, feels really creepy. I'm as wobbly as they are. Foam blobs float in front of my face, and lazy tentacles linger on my legs. I like to think they're saying a slimy yet tender hello. They're probably panicking about how hard my bones are. Then, having successfully swum in the Safe Jellyfish

Lake (NB, not the local name), I get in the sea to go snorkelling and get stung by a jellyfish.

I never get tired of sitting on the end of the jetty by my hut. In the daytime I watch the fish. At dusk I watch the sunset, staring at the sky as nothing moves but everything changes. And at night I watch the phosphorescence, imagining silent plankton discos under the glittery waves. I never want to leave, but I have to. And before I know it I'm back on the mainland, steeling myself for the long journey home.

My solo ways in Sulawesi went too fast, and I blame Time. The Master of Deception. The King of Tickery. Heading back to the real world, it feels like I've only been away momentarily – on a day trip maybe. But I haven't. It's been two months.

My first weeks away were like waking up in the morning of the metaphorical day trip: confused, out of focus, not sure what's happening. The middle month was like the actual day out: time was flying, I was having fun, and I didn't notice I was doing things because I was too busy doing them. The last week has been like bedtime: me wishing the day would last a bit longer in a childish fight against sleep. Which makes my final flight back to London the actual slumber after my long, solo excursion. My eyes shut and I think of the beginning and the purple sea and the islands waving at me. And I remember they're still out there.

There are beautiful things happening all the time. We just need to look for them.

Ella Pawlik lives in Bristol, where she peddles words for monetary favours. She spends her life saving to go travelling, actually going travelling, and then wishing she was doing it all over again. This cycle-of-a-process usually takes some time. When she's at home in the West Country she grows  misshapen vegetables, volunteers for various charities, plays the piano and talks too loudly, though not all at the same time.

My Daughter's Laugh
Dom Tulett

Walking the dusty streets around Villa de Leyva, in the Colombian Andes, I saw in a rock wall the face of my daughter's favourite toy. Days later, in the coffee fields of the country's west, her push-trike showed itself to me in a rickety wheelbarrow resting decrepit against the crumbling wall of a farmer's ancient shack. I heard her laugh in La Candelaria.

My first overseas work trip as a father took me away from her. It hadn't been planned that way; a thick cold and miserable nights kept her and my wife grounded in the UK, unable to join me for my few days of work and few weeks of holiday. Our three-week stomp around Colombia – our first significant trip as a family – had thus become an exercise in watching the clock, counting down the days, pining for home. My wife stayed behind but had encouraged me on. 'You should stay out there after work,' she said. 'Everything's paid for in any case. My parents will help here. We'll be at the airport when you get back.'

At first it felt like an opportunity, a break from the sleepless nights of home. Three weeks of exploring Colombia, with time on my hands and space in my world. But the imagined gloss quickly wore off. Before the holiday part of the trip had even begun I had lost my enthusiasm, and not even calls home could improve my mood.

I tried to fill my time in Bogotá, unhappy with the emptiness of the hotel room, but more and more moments reminded me of home and the family I had left behind. A startled bird flew from a tree and I involuntarily pointed it out with a feigned enthusiastic exclamation. I heard myself talking to no-one when I passed some colourful flowers – 'a red flower, a pink flower' – followed each time by their true name, spelt out slowly through the syllables: 'a white flower – *mag-no-li-a*'. A fruit bowl at breakfast took me back to snack times at home, and my daughter's glee when I'd prop an emptied banana skin on top of my head. That laugh again, that beautiful laugh; its absence haunted me as much as the empty cot standing conspicuously in the corner of the hotel room.

I wandered from my hotel in the Candelaria district to some of the nearby hostels. I found a bar and drank a beer. I watched couples whispering over flickering candles and groups laughing loudly around tables of empty beer cans. I had another beer. No-one else was sitting on their own. I looked around the walls of the bar and saw a sign-up sheet for a city bike tour the following morning. There was only one name on the sheet: Andreas Oskarsson, perhaps a fellow solo traveller. I added mine.

Andreas Oskarsson was from Sweden, tall and thin, with loose curls of brown hair and a long, narrow face. He wore stylish, thick-rimmed glasses, and constantly tilted his head to one side so that the glasses looked uneven and gave him the appearance of being either confused by everything that was said to him or of having not fully heard it. But he heard everything and he got everything.

I tried to stick close to Andreas on the ride – he was the only other solo cyclist – but it wasn't easy. Andreas spoke to everyone. He cycled between couples to start up conversations. He would pedal into the middle of large groups of friends, picking up whatever they were talking about. I marvelled at how he always found a natural way of connecting with other people. I assumed that people would resent me for intruding, but everyone liked – and welcomed – Andreas.

The bike tour took us around several of Bogotá's central neighbourhoods. We were shown murals of political graffiti, a 'garbage museum', which was the house of a local hermit ('He was educated in Paris…') with mountains of broken boots and wind chimes of splintered CDs, a coffee bar where two children danced and sang for money at the door. We stopped at a market. The guide showed us exotic fruits and offered us samples. Andreas was asking questions when my attention was stolen by a series of muffled bangs coming from deep within a café across the road. Customers were sitting calmly out front, suggesting the noises were normal. I nudged Andreas to look at the café.

The tour guide was cutting bite-sized pieces of a local passionfruit. Andreas asked him, 'What's going on in there?'

'It is a game,' he said. '*Tejo*. You can't go in.'

Later that day, Andreas and I played tejo, a cross between darts and *pétanque*, with gunpowder. Pressed into the centre of the soft clay game board sits an iron ring, the size of a football, with folded paper pouches propped against it. Whenever a rounded metal weight, thrown underarm down the long, narrow alley, hits one of the pouches, the gunpowder inside it explodes with a shuddering crack that rattles the walls and sends the novice player ducking for cover. My daughter would not have enjoyed this game. I asked one of the men working in the tejo alleys how much it costs to play. 'You do not pay to play tejo. You buy a crate of beers and then you play for free.' I thought that my wife might not have enjoyed this game either.

Villa de Leyva was crowded in the lead up to the Easter weekend. The tight cobbled streets heaved with an army of Colombians, mostly on their own breaks from the city, all dressed in bright yellow T-shirts. Fresh off the bus, I settled into a small café. An ornamental white cast-iron bicycle propped open the green slatted door, vibrant bunches of flowers blooming out of the basket. *Pink flower, purple flower. Car-na-tion.*

The café was full of bright yellow T-shirts. Everyone looked at me, underdressed for the occasion, as I walked through the door, then raised their eyes back up a few degrees to resume watching the television set balanced on a crooked shelf above where I stood. I ordered a beer, wedged myself on to a small wooden stool and craned my neck to watch the football – Bolivia versus Colombia. The match was being played at a high altitude, to which the Bolivian players were accustomed. The Colombians were tiring. It was not looking good for them as the game neared its end, but through heavy legs and light lungs Colombia managed to score the winning goal in the last minute.

The mood in the café, until that moment a nervous, silent, fidgety den, exploded into joy and fervour and relief. The yellow shirts welcomed me as one of their own. My appearance had changed the course of the game, apparently. Long after the final whistle we stayed and drank. Beer became wine. Wine became *guaro*, a rum-style drink served in tall, thin shot glasses, which never stayed empty or full for long. Afternoon became evening. Evening became hungover morning, my first in over a year.

Three buses took me from the mountains to the deep green fields of the Zona Cafetera, Colombia's famous coffee-growing region. In a coffee shop in Salento I met a couple who asked to share my table.

I had laid down my guidebook whilst I went to order another cup. My place saver became my ice breaker. They asked me if I was in town for the mushrooms. Apparently people travelled from all over the country and beyond to seek out the 'special' mushrooms in the fields. I had no idea about this. It wasn't in the guidebook, at least not in the chapters I had been reading over the past couple of months on travelling with children and activities for families. I had missed the good stuff.

The woman's name was Carolina and her husband was Luc. He was Canadian, she was Colombian. They both held easy relaxed smiles which told me they were happy where they were, in a comfort zone. I had started to remember what that smile was.

Luc was a natural physician, seeking herbal remedies for a range of ailments. They had bought some acres of land in the Amazon to research plants. 'You must head down there. It's beautiful country. There are *tepuis* nearby. You know, like straight-edged, flat-topped mountains. You can take an indigenous guide and hike there from our land. It's wonderful. No-one knows they're there.'

There was also a shaman I must visit, near Mocoa in the south of the country. 'He's an amazing man. Sixty years old. He'll tell you a lot about yourself. And his father still practises too. He's a hundred-and-nine. Take my email address.'

All this because I had left a book on a table. I wasn't going to sample the local mushrooms, or trek to the undiscovered tepuis, or visit a shaman four hundred miles away – not on this trip anyway – but it was thrilling to have the opportunity.

Instead, on another recommendation, I packed water and a little food, and followed a trail through the hills to a waterfall, and when I got there I sat on a rock for an hour, smiling at the endless ripples in the pool below. I thought of home, of my wife and daughter, of what they were missing and what I was missing. Reasons to be happy and reasons to be sad. Later I walked back slowly, taking everything in – the wind picking up and singing in my ears, the change in the smell of the grass as lowering rain clouds altered the atmosphere, the clumps of purple flowers. *Hi-bis-cus.* I let it rain on me, refusing to pick up my pace.

Back at the hostel I took a long shower, changed into fresh clothes and went to the bar. I looked around at the other customers. Each table held travel secrets, and it struck me that as a solo traveller I was more likely to discover those secrets than if I were travelling with my partner or as part of a family. In those group dynamics there feels less of a requirement to engage with other people – locals or fellow travellers – and you therefore don't learn those new things. I would never have played tejo if not travelling solo. I now have a shaman on recommendation. Rumours and stories and opportunities all opened up and became available, and it was completely up to me if I wished to take them.

The following week I landed back in London. Waiting at the carousel for my bag I reflected that the trip did, of course, recharge my batteries as all good travelling should. But more specifically it reinvigorated my love of travelling. I can't wait for my daughter to be old enough for us to go away somewhere and for her to appreciate those things. And when we do, we will do it as if travelling solo. We'll use the guidebook as a guide, not a bible. We'll talk to people, listen to people, take suggestions and follow rumours, even if they lead no further than the joyous, mischievous whisper of anticipation. The thought of this made me smile as I picked up my bag, walked through customs, turned into the arrivals hall, and heard my daughter's laugh.

Dom Tulett lives with his family in Harpenden. On his daily commute to London he writes stories for his daughter about the places to which he's travelled. Alongside these, he is  currently working on a novel set during the final months of the civil war in Sri Lanka. He is the 2017 winner of the New Travel Writer of the Year Award from Bradt.

A Night in Room 13
Sarah Pope

I bought the tickets to China as my wedding anniversary gift to us, and stuck them on the fridge with a smiley magnet. I was hoping for a second honeymoon, or at least a suspension of hostilities over the car repair. But the anniversary was marked by him moving in with my best friend Gloria.

I sat in the kitchen that whole weekend, in my Mickey Mouse dressing gown, stunned, staring at the tickets to China.

It was 1986 and China was an alien world. Not my first holiday choice. He was the thrill seeker. I thought he'd love it.

The clock beeped a reminder on every hour. We had been together for 364 days. Now he was gone. He wasn't coming back. I couldn't possibly tell anyone I knew. I wanted to run away.

At midnight on Sunday, I made the decision. I *would* run away. To China, where no-one knew me.

At Heathrow I joined my 'discerning travel' group. Clearly I was a novice among these veterans. My unwieldy bag slumped alongside the array of neat cases with their bright labels, little coded padlocks and raincoats strapped on top. No-one else brought hold luggage. These experienced travellers wore light, drip-dry outfits, anticipating delays and unscheduled stopovers. They seemed to be arguing about their tickets.

A tall man approached. Mr Irving. He was mature, discreet, tooth-whitened, pleased to meet me. Yes, it was my first long-haul trip. On my own. Yes, nervous. Yes, it was a big suitcase. '"Be Prepared", you know,' I said.

'Yes, you might want a padlock,' he agreed.

He laughed with an extra effort and asked about my ticket. Apparently the group was split between two flights, a day apart, from Hong Kong to *Peking*. (Mr Irving emphasised *Peking*.) Half of us would spend an extra day in Hong Kong. Not me though. I was booked on the first flight out. Mr Irving smiled more patiently at my ticket.

'Wouldn't *you* like an extra day in Hong Kong – if you haven't been before...? For the *shopping*... They speak English there, you know. Not like *Peking*. We can exchange our tickets.' He showed me his.

'No, thank you. I'd rather have more time in Beijing.'

Nonplussed, Mr Irving frowned. The ticket-swapping scrum closed ranks behind him – a tight circle of smart-casual rumps.

'*Bei-jing!*' he said, with feeling.

Beijing airport welcomed us, in the middle of the night, hours late, with low lighting and a perpetual loop of the *William Tell* Overture. A dancing shadow hurried towards us and turned into Mr Wu, our local guide. He claimed us with a bow, counting heads. 'Twelve English people, please.' We were thirteen.

Then I spotted Mr Irving. That was odd. He definitely should have been in Hong Kong for another day. I was quite sure he hadn't managed to change his ticket.

'Wait here, please.' Mr Wu indicated the far side of the terminal, below the speakers. 'The bags will come here soon,' he added and then went away, to locate a thirteenth hotel bed, I supposed.

Of course, I was the only passenger waiting for hold luggage.

I sat on the floor, staring, fixated, at the carousel, watching for the yellow stain, round and round again. And my bag, which never appeared.

Everyone else sat down, coded their little padlocks open and unpacked extra jackets and snacks.

At last, we heard faraway footsteps on the tiles. Mr Wu, in his green Western-style suit, and his female colleague, in a black Mao tunic, turned the corner. He clapped twice and beckoned.

'We go to Lee Garden Hotel.'

Everyone pushed forward, falling foul of each other's cases. Mr Wu pointed me towards his colleague. She gently took my arm.

'No problem, miss. I am Sadie, sister of guide, Mr Wu. *You* are in Beijing. Bag is in Hong Kong. Also bed is in Hong Kong.'

Mr Irving's bed, actually, I was sure. I waited, jetlagged out, while Sadie downloaded more English words.

'You come with me to Friendship Hotel. You pay taxi?'

Sadie worked at the Friendship Hotel, where the international journalists, the 'foreign experts', stayed. Officially she was a cleaner and kitchen maid, so she knew when rooms were unoccupied while the regulars were out on assignment.

The security boy at the grand entrance checked our documents. Sadie searched the rack of keys, chose number 13 and signed out.

'I come tomorrow.'

I was really on my own now with only the clothes I was wearing.

But room 13 was glorious – dark wood panelling, big Western-style bathroom, toothbrush (thank goodness), thick towels, fridge, gold silk dressing gown.

I was hungry, so I looked around for any complimentary snacks. There was a half-eaten packet of cheese sandwiches. What luck. And a thermos flask full of warm water. So delicious.

I kicked my walking boots under the bed, out of the way. Oh no! They bounced back off a pair of men's shoes already there. Wardrobe? Man's suit. Chest of drawers? Boxer shorts and socks. I was too tired to care if the owner was expected back tonight.

In what seemed to be morning, I woke up, anxious, listening. Someone in the bathroom? When I opened the door a millimetre, the faint scurrying stopped. I felt for the light switch and the wall opposite seethed with insects. Oriental cockroaches sprinted down the tiles, over the toothbrush, and disappeared below the washbasin. Bath time! Gold taps full on, I jetlagged to the deep end, defensively splashing.

My travel clothes were pretty shot by now. So much for 'Be Prepared'. Maybe I could borrow a shirt and underwear until my luggage turned up? I chose blue boxer shorts, and a striped shirt – big, but clean. Forget socks. They wouldn't fit in my shoes. Same old Wonderbra, of course, and jeans. I left some honeymoon lingerie dripping over the bath.

After that, I panicked. What if Sadie never came back? What if the room owner did, and spoke only Chinese? Maybe I would go to prison and no-one would ever know what happened.

The red telephone rang.

'You OK? Eat now?' I almost wept to hear Sadie's voice.

Sadie showed me to a table in the airy breakfast room. Two foreign experts welcomed me without prejudice. They couldn't see my underwear.

'Quick, please.' Sadie parked her twig broom.

'Too late for the full English.' One of the experts helped himself to a porcelain vase of yoghurt and a sweet bread roll. I copied him. A team of cleaners closed in on us with a clank of metal buckets.

When I was halfway down my yard of yoghurt, Sadie took it away.

'Now you go to Lee Garden Hotel, see English friends, and Mr Wu,' she said. 'There is bed for you today. One guest go.'

I made a move to collect my wet washing. Sadie barred my way to the lift.

'No, no time. Come with me.'

She unfolded a piece of paper. I could make out a grid-pattern diagram labelled: 'A simple route from Friendship Hotel to Lee Garden Hotel.' Seventeen sets of traffic lights.

At the bike rack, Sadie released a sturdy Flying Pigeon, no gears, no lights, branded in English and Chinese. She demonstrated a little bounce to straddle the crossbar. Not exactly a girlie mount.

I waited for her to check out her own bike. Instead, she pointed into the haze beyond the hotel gates.

'You go east. One hour. I work now.'

She patted my arm and hurried back into the hotel. I was on my own again.

Jetlag made this possible. I functioned in a trance. It was like stepping into an IMAX movie from the front row of the stalls. I shut my eyes and lurched into the traffic.

The unexpected weight of the Flying Pigeon shoved me sideways. A diesel truck, moulting bits of cardboard, coughed black smoke rings and sliced past with a centimetre to spare. One of the foreign experts overtook on a racing bike with gears, waving and shouting, 'Keep right – except sometimes. Watch out for bricks and missing manhole covers.'

The fast lane teemed with multitasking pedestrians – a young man tying a piece of meat to a bike frame and rolling gas bottles; a grandmother balancing a toddler at arm's length for a pee, while checking tyre pressures and lighting her pipe.

In the early morning gloom, the shoal of unlit commuter bikes flowed steadily, until a bendy bus or yellow taxi bored past on high beam, illuminating my map, and changing lanes without warning. I wobbled every time a raucous cough announced a projectile spitter within range, warming up.

At the third set of lights, the other foreign expert caught up.

'Convict parade,' he shouted, as a flatbed truck, a carnival float with five militia and a man in chains on board, crossed our path. The lights changed several times before the crowd let them through.

'Execution. He'll be shot today by firing squad.'

A very old man, taking his caged birds for an outing, leaned over to offer me pine nuts from a paper bag, and a celebratory pink feather duster.

'Thank you! *Xiè xie!*'

At the seventeenth junction, beside an iconic, willow-pattern boating lake, I glanced up, distracted by a green flashing sign – 'Lee Garden Tourist Hotel'.

I had done it! On my own! Without anyone telling me not to turn the map round like that, as I worked out the route. A kind of joy obliterated the pain in my knees. I left the Flying Pigeon to its fate and limped inside.

A bedraggled English tour group was trying on shabby old clothes in the foyer. They all had wet hair and bare feet.

But there was Mr Wu... and Mr Irving... passing round leggings, socks, towels, shirts, jumpers, pashminas and evening skirts from a huge black holdall. Mine! They saw me stagger in and froze.

'Welcome, miss! Good news,' improvised Mr Wu, overacting. 'Bag is here.' He pointed to my half-empty case.

'Bad news,' proposed Mr Irving, wearing my Mickey Mouse dressing gown, shivering. 'Boating accident. Everyone fell in. Cold. Wet… Hypothermia… You understand?'

What could I say? They were so damp and dejected, scrambling through my winter collection.

'You had a boating accident this morning? It's only coffee time now!' (I could see no coffee.)

'Oh, yes. Breakfast is six thirty every day. Scheduled activity starts at seven thirty. Boating accident was at nine thirty.'

They gave me a ragged round of applause and carried on choosing garments. I joined in. The boxer shorts were giving me blisters.

Mr Wu looked pleased. He snapped his fingers.

'Ten minutes, please, we go to Forbidden City. Bicycle tour.'

I could see Sadie outside, unloading twenty-four Flying Pigeons from a white van. I knew I would never see my wet washing again. It would forever baffle the rightful occupant of room 13 as he looked for his shirt and boxer shorts.

Sarah Pope has travelled the world as a viola player in symphony orchestras, and played with her string quartet on Mediterranean cruises. She has written reviews and features for music magazines and a violin book for beginners, *A New Tune A Day*.

A Thaw in Naples

Claire Morsman

Pop! Pop! POP!

I couldn't sleep. I felt alone and on edge, not least because of the aggressive popping of bubble gum just outside my first floor hotel window. I had earlier peeped through the dusty curtains to see, her face level with my bare feet, a prostitute. Glancing up at me with a lazy swoosh of lengthy eyelashes, she chewed on, unconcerned. Being English, and wearing a nightie, I had felt embarrassed, not least when she jiggled her half-exposed buttocks at me with a belligerent smirk. Pop!

I sighed. I found myself struggling to love Naples, or even to like it. My friend had cancelled the day before we were to fly, but I had decided to go ahead anyway. With a travel companion, I wistfully fretted, we would have seen whimsy in the everyday Italian scenes today, talked about the beauty of the city and felt safety in companionship. But I didn't have a companion. I was by myself.

Pop! Well, almost.

I lay in bed and thought about my day. Or rather, my yesterday. First, a taxi. The driver filing his nails. I climbed in and he had rubbed his hair hard, accelerated violently, then shook his head. I realised he was more interested in examining the fallen dandruff on his leather jacket than driving, so distracted myself from the danger by gaping at un-helmeted teenagers casually careering by on scooters, the ruined buildings yellowed like old teeth, the puddles of plastic rubbish and shop signs clinging with blackened Sellotape alongside rashes of graffiti.

The violence of this taxi journey due to loose or non-existent parts of the road had jolted my uptight body and my spine resisted rather than relaxed. The street hawkers, or modern-day *lazzaroni* – infamous ruffians of earlier centuries, both then and now the poorest of Naples' society – were still in evidence, laying out fake designer bags, hats and tat like chess pieces on the pavements and strategically rearranging them to attract a sale. Hail shattered down, but the sellers merely produced plastic sheets and carried on. I began to admire their tenacity, but hated the scruff, the cold and the resulting pavement disorganisation that pedestrians had to hopscotch. A part of me realised I was being unreasonable, but that only made me grumpier and harder to please.

Later, alone at the ristorante pizzeria Antonio & Antonio, I inhaled the fumes from the motorbike of passing *Carabinieri* and watched the blush and bruises of sunset, woven through by the silhouettes of birds, spreading over the *golfo*. Fishermen and islands were visible only as golden glints on the velvet ruffle of water. So *this* was the Naples I had heard about. I walked to the bay front, but there men waved, hopped off their bicycles, hissed, hovered, winked, raised eyebrows, whistled and called to me, '*Ciao bella!*' As the sun sank I felt uncomfortable and vulnerable, not least when I made it to the rocks against which the dark waves lapped to see spray-painted daubs of lewd graffiti. It began to rain as I walked home. A man followed me. I sped up. My mind continued to close against Naples and I could see nothing but things I didn't like or trust.

Near my hotel, men peed in groups outside the closed but well-lit bookshop; secretive hunched figures trudged through the puddles and cringed as the lightning exposed them. Rubbish trucks moaned and hissed. My shadow-man grew abusive as I hurried on. I hated Naples and its inhabitants and fantasised about spending the next day in the hotel.

Back in the sanctuary of my room, I had stepped out on to my oblong overlooking the Piazza Giuseppe Garibaldi and watched station workers on the concourse push individual plastic branches into a Christmas tree trunk, ready to surprise commuters in the morning. Bed. The clock ticked on and bubble gum popped somewhere just below... Pop!

The next morning, I drew back the curtains to see that the rain had cleared and that the prostitute had vanished with the dark. Refreshed, and possibly resigned, I decided to give Naples one more try. Striding out into the chaotic streets, with a confidence I was determined to feel, I caught public transport to Pompeii where I made eye contact with local fellow passengers and received smiles. Even the stern-looking man opposite me morphed into the stereotypically effusive Italian once I had mistakenly bashed him on the ankle, his large nose wrinkling with humour at my clumsy Italian apology. His warmth stayed with me as he went to great pains to reassure me where I was to get off, insisting I follow him to see the half-scrubbed-off map further down the carriage. Sitting again, he offered me an orange. I accepted, feeling nurtured, and aware that everyone nearby had been amused by and somehow supportive of our halting exchange. My vulnerability now seemed to attract goodwill rather than any predatory behaviour and I relaxed into my seat, inhaled the smell of the orange skin and absorbed the loud and excitable pre-Christmas chatter of the locals. Once there, assorted hat sellers and ticket touts perked up, but my body language said, '*Grazie*, but not today!' and they turned their attention to a few straggling tourists in couples behind me.

Pompeii alone, out of season, was the most extraordinary experience and I had the mental and physical space to will myself back to AD79. Alone in an amphitheatre. Alone in the quiet streets. Alone to imagine the Romans who had planted those vines, laid those mosaics and written that graffiti in the House of the Citharist: 'Amplicatus, I know that Icarus is buggering you. Salvius wrote this.' I smiled to myself. I was aware how lucky I was to have been able to choose my own path through such a well-visited attraction, unimpeded by anyone else's decisions or preferences.

I ate at a roadside stall and, perhaps needing to share what I had just experienced, I initiated a conversation with the Italian chap eating alone opposite me. Lunch morphed into drinks in town together where he left me to enjoy a long walk alone, happily immersed in the hoots, shouts and artisanal madness of the Spaccanapoli, especially marvellously *eccentrico* pre-Christmas with the thousands of beautifully crafted nativity *presepi* on display. Workshops and stalls brandished a million handmade miniature statues all expectantly waiting to be chosen for family Christmas scenes, from the more traditional holy figures to caricatures of present-day politicians and sportspeople, while locals' washing hung still overhead, despite the frenetic buzz in the air.

'*Ciao bella!*' I turned and smiled to acknowledge the harmless compliment from a passing cyclist; yesterday it would have seemed predatory. Finally, my guard had fallen and correspondingly my enjoyment of the city soared. Poor old Naples had initially been coloured and bruised by the bashing I had given it, but now I realised my early apprehension had been fuelled by a fear of joining in and by my awareness of being alone, defensively self conscious, being new to this way of travelling. As I'd said goodbye to my new pal – the first of many this trip – earlier that afternoon, I may not have realised it then but I was saying hello to relishing future trips by myself, when I would enjoy my own company and the chance to explore at my own pace and hear both the real peace and din of a destination.

Happily tired and back in the hotel, I drew my curtains.

Pop! Pop!

I looked through and down and grinned. The lady of the night smiled back. She was attractive and her expression friendly, I now realised, much like Naples itself.

Claire Morsman travels extensively for both work and pleasure, and is often moved to write about it. She is an international English examiner, PhD student, travel-guide researcher, professional de-clutterer, Moroccan guesthouse owner and founder of Morsbags. She is always looking forward to visiting somewhere new, and often longing to revisit somewhere she's already been. As long as she's on the move she's happy, and travelling with her toddler, Minnie, is a new excitement.

Tips

If you've old memorabilia (photos, newspaper cuttings, diaries...) about the place you're visiting, take them to show to local people. You'll give pleasure, and have a genuine reason to get into conversation. I've done this in Malta, Greece, Cambodia and the Channel Islands, with photos and books that belonged long ago to my father; onlookers delightedly stroked the grainy old pictures and reminisced about how things used to be. Schemes like stuffyourrucksack.com also help travellers to engage with the local community and contribute usefully. *Janice Booth*

Take a wooden doorstop. It's small and light to carry but can get you a good night's sleep if you're feeling vulnerable. *Claire Morsman*

It is no longer possible to register with the UK embassy abroad, but keep friends or family updated on your whereabouts, and keep some emergency cash on you. *Claire Davies*

Travelling solo makes you much more approachable – and it makes it easier for you to approach others. So speak to local people and keep an open mind; you'll make new friends and you never know where it may lead. I asked someone for directions while on a bus in Ecuador, we continued chatting and kept in touch, and a few weeks later he ended up inviting me to his brother's wedding. *Vicki Brown*

Tips

on solo cycling by **Pat Smith**

You usually don't need to book accommodation in advance, especially when camping, but *always* do so around public holidays and for Friday and Saturday nights. Even as a sole traveller with a bike and very small tent, I had trouble at times.

Warmshowers.com is a website through which keen cyclists provide free accommodation for touring cyclists. The network is denser in Europe than the UK.

Do you belong to any organisations that could give you publicity? Before I left, I wrote a short piece that was published in the University of the Third Age's magazine and ended up staying with some wonderful people.

Chocolate milk is the most wonderful rehydrating drink, more nutritious and far tastier than water.

Go on a bike maintenance course beforehand if you can.

A Big Adventure

Sometimes an exploratory trip leads to a change of career, or an idea morphs into months of physical endeavour. Katie Grayson hikes the 2,650 miles of the Pacific Crest Trail alone, while Graham Mackintosh challenges himself to walk round the coast of Mexico's Baja California although at the time he is a self-confessed couch potato. There are adventures at the beginning of one's working life and towards the end of it, both equally transformative: Anne Axel cycles around Madagascar and forges a new direction for herself, while Sheelagh Reynolds takes a granny gap year. Finally, Sally Watts buys a round-the-world ticket, leaves her job and embarks on a new life.

What if You Get Lost and Die?

Katie Grayson

If someone had told me I'd walk solo from Mexico to Canada up the west coast of the United States I would have laughed out loud.

I can't remember whose idea it had been, but I'd read the book *Wild* by Cheryl Strayed which depicted her journey on parts of the Pacific Crest Trail, a 2,650-mile hike through California, Oregon and Washington State, which hundreds of people attempt each year. A friend and I had talked about it; then my friend dropped out. I couldn't do it alone, could I? But I had too much invested in it to back out, with my visa and interview completed, flights purchased and hiking permits sought. So I signed up to walk it alone in the summer of 2015.

I'd never done anything like it before. I'd done a bit of travelling here and there, but never in the States, certainly no long-distance hikes and always with someone to share the decision making. My family and friends didn't exactly fill me with confidence. 'Why are you walking all that way?' people asked. 'What if you get lost? Fall off a cliff? Get attacked by a bear and die?' Frankly, even the thought of flying alone was almost enough to put me off. But I had to do it. No matter how scared I was by the unknown, something had stirred in me.

The immigration officer looked at me, down at my visa and back again at me. Then without speaking he stamped it and roared, 'Next!' I had six months to go anywhere in 'the land of the free'. I would have liked to have spent a few days wandering around LA, but I was already weeks behind the kick-off date, so I headed to my hostel.

Collecting the remaining items I needed in downtown LA, I boarded a double-decker train to San Diego and watched the scenery whizz by. It was scorching when I exited the air-conditioned station and made my way to the tram. Half an hour later I was waiting at the bus stop making the most of the shade. I got talking to a bus driver who was amazed that a twenty-five-year-old woman had come all the way from England to hike through America alone. He asked if I had anything to protect myself with such as a weapon. No, I replied in a small voice, feeling foolish. He then spent the next hour attempting to get me a taser, but couldn't, so instead he asked for my number and said he would be there to back me up if anything happened.

I arrived in Campo as dusk fell. I grabbed a last-minute sandwich and watched as the small town shut down for the night. I wandered aimlessly like a stray cat, having nowhere to go. I hadn't thought this part through. Walking a little way out of town, I set up camp beneath a huge tree; at least if it rained, I'd have shelter. Suddenly I saw little black dots making their way across my bag. *What the...?* Then they started crawling on me. I batted them off and started to feel pain. They were huge ants. I swiped them off as best as I could, hauled myself back over the spiky fence and ended up sleeping in someone's garden whilst the immigration vehicles patrolled constantly.

By 5 a.m. I was up and walking, too excited to sleep. The rising sun cast a glow across the land. A lone car slowed down alongside me. I got nervous as the window wound down and kept going, pretending the car was not there.

'Hey?'

I kept walking.

'Hey, are you hiking the PCT?'

I froze and turned to look. A large, dusty 4x4 was sitting next to me with a cheery lady and an older male driver inside. Two younger men were sitting in the back.

'Err, yes...'

'Well jump in,' the man said, thumbing to the rear. He turned out to be Bob, one of the trail angels who go out of their way to help hikers, asking for nothing in return. The three in his car had stayed over the previous night, relaxed and eaten, ready to start the trip. Bob took our photos and wished us well.

I spent the first day hiking twenty miles with the three others, marching under the desert sun. The forty-degree heat burned down on us. I felt safe within my group, stopping my mind from wandering negatively to the idea of temperamental rattlesnakes slithering their way into my sleeping bag later. In fact, I slept soundlessly.

My body was a wreck the next morning. Determined to keep my mileage high I set off at first light. Snoozing sounds floated over me as I clipped my bag shut and tiptoed silently away. The sun rose on my right as I motored through the undergrowth. Twenty miles down, 2,630 to go.

On my second night, I fell asleep beneath a star-covered sky and awoke drenched by low clouds. Wrapping myself in my outer tent I tried to sleep on, but couldn't, so I got up and did the only thing I could – hike. I'd managed a mile before the weather became so bad that I decided to turn back. I hit the main road and found a campsite. I was about to get a drink from the taps when I saw a sign:

DANGER E COLI PRESENT

Defeated, I headed to the shower block to warm up but found it locked. I huddled in the doorway before deciding to walk to the village. It was a five-mile hike and fog had rolled in magnificently while rain blasted me from all sides. At least I was getting warmer from the movement. Cars passed and one pulled up beside me. I slowed, cautious as the passenger door opened. I peered in and saw a man beckoning me inside. He cleared some room from his packed-out seat and turned the heating up.

'I live in the village. I can take you there,' he said and in I hopped, forsaking all I'd ever been told about stranger danger. It turned out that the man, Dave, owned the mountain-gear shop and helped out hikers. We arrived at his store, which was brimming with gear, and he started up his wood-burning stove and placed a kettle in the middle to make me a hot chocolate complete with marshmallows. I couldn't believe my luck! By the afternoon the storm had gone and I was able to continue my epic journey.

The first seven hundred miles consisted of trudging through deserts with long stretches between water. In times to come I would look back on this part with affection. However, it would have to bow down to the Sierra Nevada stretch which blew my mind, even though it was bear country and I had to carry a two-pound bear canister to protect my food, and the mosquito population never gave me a break. Despite what it threw at me, it contained the most jaw-dropping beauty I'd ever laid my eyes on. The water was plentiful, pure and clear, and I'd often drink straight from the river. Deer ambled by, aware of but unperturbed by my presence.

The views from the tallest peaks were panoramic and endless and kept me gaping for hours. I'd navigate myself through the remote wilderness and sometimes not see a human, roads or any sign of civilisation for days. This didn't worry me. I loved it. When did that happen? I began to live by the trail motto: 'Hike your own hike': go at your own pace, stop when you're tired, eat when you're hungry, sleep when you want, night hike if you fancy it. It was just me and the wilderness beginning our own little private love affair. Every day I'd tramp through its earthy woods, touch the century-old bark, sing for the pleasure of it and sleep in the golden silence. Just the two of us.

One of the hardest moments was after I'd taken a two-week holiday off-trail with a friend and her parents-in-law. We went surfing at Venice Beach and travelled to a hippie festival in Oregon. They treated me as one of their own. At the end of the holiday they drove four hours to get me back on the trail, then hugged and kissed me goodbye. I waved till they were out of sight and then I broke down in tears. It was an overwhelming surge of emotions for these people who had encouraged my endeavours and cheered me on. And here I was, blubbering, with 950 miles down, 1,700 left to go.

It took me a while to reacclimatise to the hiking way of life. At one point I got off the trail for two days and debated whether to quit and sightsee America with my remaining money. I tried to get a friend to join me, but they declined. I'm glad they did as it forced me to shake myself down and return to the trail once again.

It took me four months to hike it. I was a walking machine. Each day I'd chew up miles and spit out ten of them by 10 a.m. – ten by ten. My body was leaner and fitter than it had ever been.

I don't know at which mile I became a hiker. Maybe I was always a hiker, but at which mile did I learn to shed my fear of being alone? The desire to hike flowed through me, willing me onwards, urging me to keep going. I could do this, I could and I would. It expelled any murmur of uncertainty from me and I grew. My mind accepted the bliss of solitude, as did my body.

When did I begin to love the solitude? Trust in my own independence? Thrive on the desire propelling me forward? I don't recall the exact moment. It all just fell into place. Amazed that I loved to cowboy camp – no tent, only a sleeping bag under the stars – it soon felt like the most natural thing in the world. Even in bear country. When did I become so fearless (or maybe naïve)?

It was only when I'd finished that it hit me: yes, you did that all by yourself, you, and you loved it. Sometimes it still feels like I dreamt it, but no, it happened. I often flick back through my journal, reading it and gazing at the tucked-in receipts and miscellaneous tickets. Then I close my eyes to picture and relive my journey. It was mine. No-one could take it away from me.

Katie Grayson is an explorer from Yorkshire in her late-twenties who is always ready for the next adventure. She became an accidental solo traveller when she took it upon herself to hike across the United States of America. She has road-tripped to the corners of Europe, island-hopped and border-crossed through south and east Asia and  is currently on a working holiday visa in Japan. Previous jobs include pop-up cinema steward, PA and laboratory assistant. She also enjoys crocheting, baking, photography and urban exploration.

Beginning
Anne C. Axel

I was twenty-one, a college senior applying to medical school, when I chanced upon a used magazine with an article about Madagascar, a place so alluring I could not put it out of my mind. I had to go there.

During the next few months I devoured every piece of information I could find about the island and its magnificent wildlife. In the age before internet, my search was slow going. But I eventually located a handful of articles and books including the Bradt guide. I studied it page by page, imagining myself exploring all those places. I acquired a large map of the island, traced potential routes with my fingers lingering on vast expanses of forest.

The more I learned about Madagascar the more consumed I became. There was a connection that I couldn't fully understand, but I believed in it so strongly that I did the unforgiveable. Instead of going to medical school I chose to follow a calling to a place I could, as yet, only imagine.

I had no practical skills to bring to such an ambitious journey. I had grown up in a household nearly devoid of outdoor activities. There'd been no hiking, camping or birding.

But I longed to fully engage with the wildness of Madagascar. I wanted to backpack through small towns, camp in the rainforest, snorkel in the Indian Ocean, photograph cheeky lemurs.

And I wanted to do it on my own terms, at my own pace. I moved in with my mother, took a retail sales position, and began saving money for my big adventure. It was easy to imagine such a bold journey from the table over which I had strewn my maps and materials, but there were moments of clarity when I realised I could never manage such an expedition on my own. Seriously. I couldn't pitch a tent and even if I could, I doubted I had the fortitude to sleep in one alone.

In fact, I lacked confidence in my ability to do any of it. Painfully shy and an introvert to boot, I had never even marshalled the courage to attend a meeting, much less an outing, of the college hiking club. Instead, I read magazine reviews of the best outdoor gear and wondered how I might ever learn to use it all. Luckily, I stumbled on to an outdoor adventure course being taught at the local community college – the potential anonymity of the classroom experience being much more appealing than the hiking club. We hiked, rock climbed, river rafted and camped. I learned to read a map, light a camping stove, filter water and shit in the woods. I gained confidence. I made a couple of friends and continued hiking, backpacking and mountain biking after the semester ended. And I realised the true value of that mountain bike. That's how I would explore the 'Great Red Island'.

By now, my family realised that I would not be deterred. I took a second job to save more money while my friends started 'real' jobs, entered graduate school, finished graduate school, got married and did all those things one does in one's early twenties. Whenever asked about my plans beyond retail and food service, I would say only that I was going to Madagascar. I started bike camping. I learned to take apart and rebuild the bike, planned my route and began a search for a travelling companion. I certainly couldn't undertake this journey on my own. I took out classifieds in an adventure travel magazine and

I did receive letters from interested parties. One came to visit and we backpacked near my home to test our compatibility. He had already cycled in many countries, including Madagascar, and it seemed the perfect match. But work beckoned him back to Texas, and after three years of searching, I still had no prospects.

Yet I carried on, ever hopeful that I would locate a fellow 'Madaphile' by my proposed departure date of autumn 1994 – four years after I'd first read that article. And when I had acquired the necessary equipment, skills and money, but there was still no prospect of a companion, I was suddenly faced with a heart-wrenching decision: I would go alone or I would not go at all.

I wrote a letter to Hilary Bradt, author of my guidebook, and asked for her thoughts on a young female embarking on a bike trip alone around Madagascar. Her hand-written response was a game changer. With her encouragement, I found the strength to believe I might be able to do this on my own. And more importantly, it helped allay my mother's fears. My mother couldn't bring herself to forbid her only child to make the trip alone, but she made no effort to hide her anxiety and unease with the idea. She was the only child of overly protective middle-aged parents who had banned such everyday activities as snow skiing, so I understood that much of her concern was simply instinctive.

I sat aboard the plane on the day of departure with my bike and mountain of belongings stowed below, and I wanted only to disembark. I felt a fear I had never known in the planning stage. My confidence melted away there in that airline seat. I was so very scared.

During my layover in Paris, I met some fellow travellers and one very kind soul, a Canadian anthropologist, took me under her wing.

When we arrived in Antananarivo she suggested we share a taxi to a nearby hotel. I shadowed her around town for my first few days, but by day five, I was well and truly on my own. I pulled all the pieces of my bike out of the transport box to begin assembly and immediately had a panic attack as I struggled to remember how it all went back together.

I flew all my gear to the northernmost city in Madagascar with the plan to cycle back to the capital – a distance of a thousand kilometres. Once in Antsiranana, I loaded up the bike for a test run south along Route Nationale 6. Just outside town I was picking up speed when I realised my bike was too unwieldy. There was just too much stuff. But I found comfort in all that 'non-essential' gear – tools, spare parts, photo equipment – and I was sickened by the mere thought of abandoning any of it. Still pedalling, I reasoned that a sensible person would abandon the spare camera, flash, tripod and loads of film. But, as a budding photographer, I could not jettison my most treasured gear. Then, suddenly, I fixated on the photography equipment. I could not lose it. Was I a target with all this stuff? Would I be robbed on the first leg of my tour and then left with no means to photograph the magnificence of this wild place? My initial frustration was quickly replaced first by fear and panic, and then by a feeling of certain defeat.

I faced a critical decision. I had either to commit fully to the adventure of the overland journey without the equipment I'd so carefully selected for photographing nature, or else prioritise my desire to photograph forests and lemurs. I spent three days in bed, in a deep depression, agonising over my incongruous goals.

I chose to immerse myself in nature. I hired a local guide and headed to the nearby national park, Ankarana Special Reserve, where I saw my first lemurs, hiked through a grand cave to an isolated pocket of dry deciduous forest, and climbed limestone karst formations called *tsingy*.

I felt great shame and disappointment in abandoning my plan to cycle overland. I did, however, manage to satisfy my desire for adventure by taking some week-long cycling trips that required less gear.

In the end, I spent four glorious months travelling solo around Madagascar, partly by bicycle, declining opportunities to travel with other tourists. While I enjoyed the company and the security, I derived more pleasure from the opportunity to linger where I wanted. And seldom was I actually alone, as the Malagasy are so very friendly. One day while cycling to a historic palace fifty kilometres distant from the main road, I encountered some deep patches of mud. Local villagers, openly astonished by the appearance of a female *vazaha*, or foreigner, pushing a strange sort of bicycle, helped me get my bike through the thick mess. In the small town near the palace, the local doctor and his family took me in for the night.

There were times when I was afraid. In the small town of Betioky, in southern Madagascar, I tried to arrange transport by ox cart to a small reserve and a kindly woman assured me, in broken French, that I would be safe venturing out into the bush with two men. Bush-taxi rides were often frightening. There was the time the lug nut was stripped beyond repair and the driver kept adding foil to help secure the wheel on the vehicle. Another time a caravan of drivers imagined they were driving a road rally at night, in the rain, along a windy road. Once I hitched a ride in the covered back of a pick-up. In the next town, the driver stopped and invited the villagers and his two drunken passengers to peer in. I felt like a caged animal at the zoo.

I feared I would be mugged or worse. But I was delivered safely to my requested destination.

Altogether I spent weeks camping in forests photographing nature and this made me intensely happy. I was intrigued and captivated by all the components of these varied ecosystems. It was in the forests that I finally realised what would be my next steps in life. I would return to school to study conservation science.

My final cycling trip was on the small Île Sainte Marie. The location was ideal for cycling and I travelled the length of the island over the first few days. Then I learned of a remote hotel on the east coast, from where I could take a *pirogue* to a secluded beach on the Indian Ocean. I set out with a small hand-drawn map along a road thickly entrenched in beach sand. I spent a glorious day alone on the white sand beach on the azure sea. A couple days later I came down with dysentery. I lost control of my bowels. Water and food went directly through me. I was terribly sick and alone at this remote hotel that had no vehicle. Ultimately, the dysentery brought my journey to an abrupt end. After receiving help in the capital I was sent to Kenya for additional treatment and from there to the United States.

Though sad to leave Madagascar, I realised this was not the end of the journey, but just the beginning. I entered graduate school and returned to Madagascar two years later for an even more epic trip – six months humping a backpack through the eastern rainforests mapping the distribution of the largest living lemur, the indri. There followed more graduate school and several more years of research in southern Madagascar.

Now, nearly twenty-five years after reading that life-changing article, I teach ecology and conduct research in Madagascar.

Clearly that journey to Madagascar has had a significant influence on my professional life, but it has been in my personal life where I have felt the greatest impact. The confidence and self-assuredness I developed while travelling alone in Madagascar have seen me through every difficulty since.

Anne C. Axel often gets to chase lemurs for a living. As an ecologist studying the abundance and distribution of lemurs in Madagascar, she spends months at a time moving between forest patches to locate and count members of these endangered species. When not in the field, Anne mentors students, teaches and writes academic publications at Marshall University in West Virginia. Anne received graduate degrees in wildlife ecology from Yale University and Michigan State University.

No Way Back

Graham Mackintosh

In the early 1980s, I could have safely described myself as a hard-baked couch potato, one whose only real talent seemed to be catering to his own comfort and safety.

Thus I surprised myself and a few others when I boldly declared that I was going to quit my job teaching at West Kent College and walk alone around Mexico's rugged Baja California peninsula surviving off the sea and the desert. Normally such resolve would have lasted about as long as it took the first drop of blood or sweat to hit the desert sand, but I had foolishly (or perhaps wisely) shared my intentions with several local newspapers, a few radio stations and even on a BBC 'nationwide' television programme.

Driving away from the studios through the rush-hour traffic, I found myself laughing. Tension release? No, I suspect it was from just looking back over what I'd done: newspapers, radio, television. I had accumulated a mountain of equipment, been given money. I'd got all that and I hadn't done a thing. It seemed so incredibly funny. I had not taken one step on my journey, yet I was 'famous'. All because of what I said I was going to do.

There was no question of going back on my word – an Englishman's word is his bond, even if he is half Scottish and half Irish. In spite of my fears I'd rather have died than feebly allow my vision to fizzle out. I had deliberately manoeuvred myself into a no-way-back situation.

Realising that in just a few days I'd be alone struggling to stay alive in a baking hot wilderness, I made a last review of the dangers before me. These included rattlesnakes, scorpions, venomous spiders, stingrays, sharks, toxic fish and shellfish, needle-spined cacti, agonising glare, tropical storms and hurricanes, flash floods, pounding surf, huge tides, rabid animals, dehydration and mental collapse. The more I read the more anxious I became, so the more I read… and the more I collapsed into a terrifyingly dark pit of negativity.

In April 1983, lonelier than I'd ever been in my life, burdened with a troubled mind, carrying a backpack that I could barely pick up, I hitched my way south from Los Angeles into Mexico.

Crossing the border at the city of Mexicali, I found myself walking down one of its more crowded shopping streets carrying my backpack with tent and sleeping bag emerging a foot on either side. A sense of paranoia came easily as cars, buses and faces flashed by. The pack and my bright red hair did a fine job of calling attention to myself. I resolved to walk about four miles to the edge of the city, to where a highway took off for my starting point – San Felipe – on the Sea of Cortez.

The city miles seemed never-ending. The day grew hotter and I wasn't sure if the tingling in my face was due to the sun or to embarrassment. My arms and neck felt tight and burned. Sweat stung my eyes. My head began to ache and no matter how much I drank I was continually thirsty. The water in my canteen turned warm and sickly. I began to feel dizzy. Anxious about throwing up or even collapsing on the footpath, I took refuge in a dingy alley. Huddled there in my misery, I feared I had taken on something I was physically incapable of finishing.

A family of Mexicans appeared from one of the houses. After a few awkward moments, I picked up my pack, mumbled something about it being hot and walked out into the stifling heat.

Somehow I made it to the junction and secured a ride with two good Samaritans from San Francisco, who had to re-pack their car to fit me in. What a joy to just sit down and be chauffeured. I was offered a cold beer and couldn't believe how good it tasted. After a burst of friendly conversation the beer and the heat seemed to catch up on us. We drifted into our own worlds.

My mood turned sombre as we crossed the flat expanse of the so-called 'Desert of the Chinamen', forty-three of whom had set out to walk from San Felipe to Mexicali in search of work. Only seven made it. The rest died of thirst. The sun-baked mountains of Baja rose before us red and seemingly devoid of life. My self-doubt intensified. *What have I done? This land does not tolerate fools.*

At last in San Felipe, I still felt somewhat delicate as I wandered around the darkening, dusty streets of town. Loud American laughter drifted in and out of my consciousness, as did indecipherable snatches of Spanish. Mexican music wafted from a dozen bars and alleyways, sweeping me along into a whirlpool of sadness. Although hungry, I could not be tempted by the street-side sellers of tacos and tamales. As I trudged back to my tent, three dogs emerged from the dust and the darkness, barking and snapping at my heels. The whole universe was mocking me and my crazy idea. The strength and bravado that had brought me that far had totally deserted me. The prospect of weeks and months alone in the desert terrified me.

Safe in my tent, I listened to the waves and stared at the fabric-softened image of the moon. I didn't want to think. Every chain of thought had a depressing conclusion. It was easier to lie on my back.

But why did I feel so miserable and inadequate? None of what afflicted me accounted for the depth of my feelings. More likely the psychological onslaught had begun. This is what I'd read about and prepared for. I now understood it in all its emotional reality. Lying there in my tent I could feel why 'despair was the greatest killer of all'. I had to break its hold.

I needed a friend. Yet there was no-one. All the old assumptions, securities and props had been stripped from me. Tomorrow it would be just me, my word, my few possessions and my bruised morale against a terrifying uncertainty.

Mumbling the words of some half-remembered hymn, tears ran down my cheeks. I promised myself that tomorrow or the next day or the next, all this madness would seem ridiculous. I forced myself to say, 'Just keep going for one week.' I knew if I could put that one week behind me, I would see it through to the end.

Mercifully, I survived the physical and psychological shocks of those first days and, knowing I had no choice, just got on with it.

I was still getting on with it more than eighteen months later. I was three-quarters of the way around the coast of Baja, scrounging enough water to survive, reasonably content with my diet of fish, clams, seaweed, rattlesnake, cactus and occasional sumptuous plates of lobster, fish, rice and beans offered by the local fishermen.

That unexpected kindness and hospitality was one of the joys of the trip, and helped make my time alone more comfortable. There was still tension and heightened awareness. I had to think of everything myself – especially of what could go wrong – but by now I was revelling more in the astonishing beauty around me and how much living one could pack into twenty-four hours. The prospect of returning to the 'real world' grew increasingly scary.

I still had to do over four hundred miles of the southern Pacific coast of Baja California, relatively flat with low headlands and mangrove swamps. Convinced my back had suffered enough carrying a sixty-to-seventy-pound pack, and craving companionship after hundreds of nights solo camping in the desert, I made another out-of-the-blue resolution – I decided to buy a *burro*, or donkey.

My previous experience with animal care was limited to a hamster. But burros seemed to be abundant. In the little oasis mission town of San Ignacio, after a long day of searching and negotiating, I parted with thirty dollars and found myself the proud if somewhat apprehensive owner of a sweet-looking white male burro that I named Bonny. The seller threw in a length of frayed rope and a worn and ancient pack saddle for fifty cents. By starlight, I led my dumbfounded companion back to my campsite in the date palms.

After a challenging week of learning the ropes and getting to know my amigo, Bonny and I were inseparable. One day, braying pitifully, he became stuck up to his belly in mud and quicksand. I thought I'd lost him. Frantically digging, pulling his rope and pleading with him to 'Push, push,' I finally got him out and unashamedly threw my arms around his neck and held him tight, our hearts beating and our bodies trembling in unison.

Had I really vowed when I bought him that there was no way I'd be sentimental with this animal? I hadn't reckoned on the power of shared hardship and danger, and the bond forged by long, lonely nights listening to the hair-raising howls of the coyotes.

Together, we dealt with everything that Baja could throw at us. And for four months we ambled along towards the end of the peninsula and the end of my journey.

Bonny and I spent our last morning together on the dazzling white sands a few miles north of Cabo San Lucas. I woke early and listened to my radio till dawn. Having put behind me the best part of two years, three thousand miles and seven pairs of boots, it was sadly ironic to hear a Los Angeles radio station urging its listeners to vacation in Baja – 'daily flights to La Paz, Loreto and Cabo San Lucas... or drive from the border to the tip... it's never been easier to get to Baja California...'

Bonny and I lay together on the beach in the early morning sun, at peace with ourselves, our universe and each other. Handfuls of coarse white sand slipped through my fingers as I muttered something about him being the best burro in the world, and thanked him for all his help and assistance over the past difficult months... Packed and ready, we dragged our tired and thirsty bodies along the final mile of beach before cutting over the hills and down towards the booming hotels and big cruise ships of Cabo San Lucas.

I thought back to the first mile I'd walked from San Felipe, and how alone and frightened I'd felt in the face of a burning vastness that seemed to be mocking each pathetic little step along the sand. I had carried on because I'd felt that I was answering the call of something much bigger than my fears. And here I was. In an hour or two the end would be in sight. Then I would have the rest of my life to try to figure out what it was all about.

Graham Mackintosh is the author of four books on Baja California: *Into a Desert Place*, *Journey with a Baja Burro*, *Nearer my Dog to Thee* and *Marooned With Very Little Beer*.

The Road to Srinagar and Beyond
Sheelagh Reynolds

Much to my surprise I ran headlong and happily into my sixth decade. I had become accustomed to a life lived alone. My marriage had ended some years previously, my children had left home, my parents had left this earth and my beloved dog had lifted his leg for the last time to wind up the neighbours by peeing on their gateposts.

I enjoyed my job running the early pregnancy clinic at my local hospital. Always challenging, sometimes joyful, often sad – I anticipated going to work with something akin to excitement, not knowing what the day would bring. I was my own boss and my colleagues were my second family. But there were clouds bubbling up on the horizon. Out of the blue a higher being was brought in to dictate my modus operandi. I lost my autonomy overnight and felt frustrated and resentful.

On top of that, my health became an issue. Gynaecological operations came hot on the heels of having my gall bladder removed. On the road to recovery, a fall in the garden left me contemplating my fractured tibia poking out into the summer's day. Finally, my heart went out of sync. Two trips to St George's later, and following an ablation, I decided there was more to life than either being stuck in a job which had lost its gloss or else in a hospital bed. But what to do?

Having announced a 'granny gap year' as the solution, I was filled with fear and excitement in equal measure. Not naturally brave, certainly not stoical, I spent sleepless nights leading up to my departure. I was petrified of flying, reduced to tears by spiders and cockroaches and feared food poisoning on bus journeys. I was terrified of snapping bones, heart arrhythmias and wasps, having suffered an anaphylactic reaction to a sting in the past. I was scared by thunderstorms. I had a new grandson and I didn't want to leave my family. And although I lived alone, I was a sociable sort and I dreaded my own company. This adventure was going to test me – with just me on the journey, would me and I get along?

Twelve months later, I had come a long way. I had volunteered in the Galápagos, explored the high Andes and sailed through storms on the Caribbean Sea. I had been badly bitten and infected by unseen insects and poisoned by food. Sleeping in the desert, I had thought I might die of cold. I had peered through the open seams in the fuselage of a tiny, current-tossed plane at the barren landscape below. In Myanmar my train had derailed in the middle of a forest fire. In Varanasi I had nearly fallen off a parapet into the flames already occupied by another body at a burning ghat.

My travels had been fairly random, taking me off-piste on a whim, but I had booked a flight home from Delhi at the end of May. However, the Himalayas were beckoning – this could be my last chance, and so with two weeks left on my visa I headed north into the mountains to McLeod Ganj, home of the Dalai Lama, where the air was pleasingly cool and the pace slow. Now with just one week left there was still time for more – and it seemed that a risky adventure into a war zone was the only suitable way to complete my trip.

And so it was that, no longer a wuss, I found myself boarding a bus for Kashmir, despite being told it was possibly dangerous. I chatted to myself companionably and popped a valium to calm me for what I knew would be a long journey over perilous, unforgiving mountain passes in a dodgy vehicle on something that would not be called a road in most places.

So narrow and tortuous was the Jammu-Srinagar National Highway that when I was there, the traffic was one way, travelling in alternate directions on designated days. Trucks occupied the inner lane and smaller vehicles, like ours, took the outer, about-to-fall-off-the-cliff lane.

Countless collapsed bridges fallen into deep ravines testified to the fact that this was a major earthquake zone. Hundreds of vehicles travelled nose to tail, constantly ferrying goods in and out of Kashmir. It was mostly construction equipment and food; and many chicken lorries, the poor, scraggy white birds with beaks gaping in distress, so cramped they looked half dead – the ones that weren't already fully dead. One of our standstills found us next to a bee lorry and the bees were making a bid for freedom. Our minibus was coated with the creatures and it was dark and stifling inside the metal box, the windows shut and no air conditioning. I had my Epipen at the ready to counter anaphylaxis should I get stung.

Slowly, slowly, stopping and starting, we gained altitude, winding our way through the harsh, craggy environment, accompanied all the while by nomadic tribes driving their flocks of goats and sheep and herds of horses up to lush summer pastures. The beasts were painfully thin after their winter in Jammu, the herders lithe and sinewy, clothed in multiple, flapping layers, their heads wound about with ragged cloths. The women were tiny and totally covered apart from their brown faces, often with babes on their backs, and children scampered along trying to keep up. All were intent on chivvying the animals along, whacking them with sticks should they pause to tear at a mouthful of scrub, weaving in and out of the traffic and hollering encouragement or maybe warning. The animals bellowed in response and the lorries honked and music blared from open windows.

What a life. Maybe they were happy – how could I tell? But at journey's end I did not envy them and the more I saw, the more I appreciated all I had left behind. I was ready to go home.

We passed many breakdowns caused by overheated engines and punctures. The drivers seemed untroubled by their predicament, standing about smoking and drinking tea, laughing in the midst of the mayhem. Where help was to come from, or how it would reach them, heaven knows. We saw more than a few serious casualties where vehicles had gone over the edge despite the many warnings along the route, written in English: 'Drive like hell and you'll soon be there,' 'This is a highway not a runway – don't take off,' and my favourite – 'Don't be silly on the hilly.'

Up and over these Himalayan passes, the scenery was stunning. Vertiginous slopes, gashed and scarred by landslides, dropped to grassy valleys where rivers, grey-green and dancing with rapids, rushed on their way to some distant ocean, swollen by the hundreds of waterfalls cascading down the mountainsides to join the ride. Several large boulders occupied the road, one as big as a double-decker bus. But the sky was blue; there was no sign of rain to further shift the landscape, and the ground was quiet and still. More than that, I had learnt to accept *que sera sera*.

From war-torn, dirty, flood-damaged Srinagar I travelled on and up to Aru in the high Kashmiri meadows. Tossing in my bed at home before my epic journey began a year ago, I could never have imagined even in my wildest dreams that I would at journey's end find myself quite alone in a village of such beauty and tranquillty, nestled between towering peaks with tall conifers reaching to the snowline.

The sole guest at the guesthouse, I had the undivided attention of Bashir, the owner. Potentially I could have been raped, robbed, murdered even, and no-one to come to my rescue for no-one knew where I was in that faraway place. Yet I feared him not. I had learned to take people at face value and his face was honest and kind. We walked through meadows peopled by shepherds, the turf warm and bouncy under our bare feet, spangled with daisies and Day-Glo purple flowers. In the afternoon we went fishing, Bashir wading into the bounding river to balance on a boulder and land an enormous fish for dinner. I sat on the bank, enchanted with the scene and at peace.

Suddenly, out of nowhere, the clouds gathered and thunder echoed off the mountains, booming and terrifying. Lightning sparked horizontally between the mountain peaks. Hail slammed through the trees, relentlessly battering me almost to the ground. Now I was afraid. Perhaps I was not going to make it home after all, and not because of dangerous journeys nor encounters with strangers, but due simply to weather. But Bashir grabbed my hand and dragged me up the hill and home to safety, heart pounding against my ribs and lungs struggling from the altitude.

Teeth by now chattering with cold and soaked to the skin, I was given a long woollen robe to change into and, as I sat on the floor with knees bent, a 'winter wife', a small charcoal brazier, was popped under my skirt. The fire blazed in the makeshift oil drum wood burner in the middle of the room and we ate fish and chips, licking the grease from our fingers as the storm continued to rage outside.

Later, I cleaned my teeth and considered how satisfying it was to wash my feet at the same time for there was no pipe attached to the sink outlet. I sank into my soft feather bed heaped with blankets and reflected on the amazing time I'd had. Not only had I seen so many incredible sights that could have been lifted straight from the pages of *National Geographic*, but also I'd met many wonderful people along the way, people I would not have given the time of day had I had a companion. I was still petrified of flying, reduced to tears by spiders and cockroaches, terrified of snapping bones and wasps and thunderstorms, but I'd done it. I had managed pretty well with just me on the journey, but aloneness had made me reach out where I would not have previously and I was amply rewarded. I drifted off with a big self-satisfied grin on my face.

Following a run of medical problems, **Sheelagh Reynolds** retired from running the Early Pregnancy Unit at the Royal Surrey County Hospital in Guildford and took off for a 'granny gap year' backpacking around South and Central America, the Far East and India. Born and brought up in Jersey, she attended university in Hull and subsequently lived in Hong Kong and New Zealand for a number of years before settling in the UK in 1987. She has three children, three grandchildren and two guinea pigs.

Going it Alone
Sally Watts

I signed my divorce papers in a hut in Sarawak. For two weeks the envelope had lurked at the bottom of my rucksack, out of sight and mostly out of mind. But the next day Meena, my friend and London neighbour, was flying home and the papers had to go too. In anticipation, and with some difficulty, we bought a bottle of wine in the largely 'dry' town of Kuching before catching our boat to Bako National Park. Outside the hut, the sun was setting and the evening rain was pounding on the corrugated iron roof, the only other sound coming from proboscis monkeys crashing through the trees. I opened the envelope, scanned the papers, took a swig of vinegary wine from a plastic mug and signed. No tears, no regrets, some sadness but also excitement about the future.

Seven months earlier, when I set off on my 'get away from it all' break, it was a different story. After a difficult separation from my ex, I wanted to escape; I needed a change. Travelling had always been my passion and I started to broach the subject with friends. In the past I had travelled with family or friends, with a group on adventure holidays or as a volunteer with a medical organisation. I wanted a travel companion; but as a nurse I could take time off and be guaranteed a job on return, a luxury many of my friends could not enjoy. I soon realised that if I was going on this trip it would be alone. I was reluctant at first, but a particularly bad day at work prompted me to rethink; I couldn't think of a reason not to go, so I handed in my notice there and then. The next day I bought a round-the-world ticket.

Two months after my fortieth birthday I was on a plane flying to India, alone and terrified. The weeks before I left had flown by, renting out my flat, sorting out visas and finances and saying too many goodbyes. After a tearful airport farewell it was with a sense of relief I boarded the plane, but hours later as I looked down over the unknown I felt sick with a mixture of excitement and fear.

The first month in India was a bit of a blur and seems like a dream. A friend of a friend was going to be in Kerala at the same time as me so we met up and it made those first few days of being alone so much easier. Of course it didn't take me long to realise I was not alone. In addition to the one billion-odd inhabitants of India there was a plethora of fellow travellers. They came in all guises and, as I learned along the way, they travelled for a multitude of reasons. I was worried that I would stand out as a lone traveller, but that fear was unfounded; there were plenty of us. Overcoming my natural English reserve and starting up conversations with total strangers wasn't easy at first, but I realised it was going to be a very lonely trip if I didn't. Soon the standard questions, 'Where are you from?', 'Where are you going?' and 'Have you been to…?' became second nature. As I grew more confident and comfortable being alone, I learned to opt out occasionally and enjoy the solitude.

There are many people on the trip whom I associate with a place. For me it was the people and the experiences that stick in my memory.

My thirty-hour train journey from Delhi to Darjeeling would not have been the same without meeting Lela, a teacher from Delhi. She spoke a few more words of English than I did Hindi so we gestured and hand-signalled our way through the journey. At regular intervals she offered me delicious titbits from a bottomless bag that never left her sight – chapattis still warm several hours into the journey, curries and other battered delicacies. When we stopped at a station I replenished the stocks under her careful guidance, a nod for yes, a scowl for no, and always-delicious sweet *chai* from the *chai wallah*. We parted as silent friends; we hugged knowing that we were unlikely to ever see each other again.

I met Sven, a traveller from Sweden, on a Saturday night in Munnar, a tea-plantation town in southern India. It was payday for the workers and by early evening the town was awash with local home-brewed liquor, the workers staggering through the streets in various states of inebriation. I beat a hasty retreat to the guesthouse and Sven and I sat on the roof looking over the endless, regimented rows of tea plants. Before long we were chatting like old friends; it felt like we had known each other for years. There were many similarities in our lives and our random meeting felt like fate. There was no romance; but we spent a couple of days walking and talking and when we said goodbye I felt I had taken a big step forward in the healing process.

It took me three attempts to leave India: overbooked flights meant trips out to the airport and a waiting game. Four months in India had taught me the art of patience and instead of being upset I just headed off to a different part of the country to explore further.

Thailand seemed calm after India and I enjoyed periods of being alone interspersed with travelling with others. I began to look further off the beaten track, avoiding the backpacker hostels and where possible staying with local families in small guesthouses. I learned to cook Thai food, took a Thai massage course, visited temples, took hundreds of photographs and would go for days without thinking about home. On Koh Samui I met Barbara, an American woman, well into her sixties and several times divorced. We laughed until we cried about the exploits of her various husbands and life in general. Travel therapy at its best.

By the time I reached Laos I was enjoying travelling alone. I loved being able to make unilateral decisions, acting on a whim and frequently changing my entire itinerary in twenty-four hours. I intended making a brief trip to Laos en route to Vietnam, but I stayed for two months and never made it to Vietnam. This was 1999 and the country was dogged with a history as a dumping ground for UXO, unexploded ordnance, courtesy of the Vietnam War. The country was just opening up to tourism and the first charter flights were landing in the capital, Vientiane. I found the Laotian people's attitude to its new visitors refreshing – friendly but not pushy; if you want to stay, fine, but if you don't, that's fine too. This was such a contrast to India and Thailand where in the big tourist destinations constant hassling and haggling could get annoying.

There was a different atmosphere in Laos and, while communication was difficult, I got by with the aid of a small, handwritten phrase book. Visiting the food markets was an eye-opener: baskets of frogs and insects and deep-fried rodents. There were huge mounds of sticky rice for breakfast, lunch and dinner. After a month of exploring the main sights in the north I headed south by boat to the remote area of Don Khong. Sitting on the roof of the boat I passed small villages and rice paddies and there was no evidence of tourism. This was my first real 'away from it all' travel.

I lived for two weeks in a hut overlooking the Mekong River and I felt comfortable just having some peace and quiet. I borrowed a bicycle and spent every day cycling into small villages and through the countryside, having 'speechless' chats with the villagers. The children helped me with their language and I taught them a few English words. One of the few travellers in the area was a Greek girl called Marianna, and one night over a couple of glasses of the potent local rice whisky we decided cycling was the way to travel. Discovering that we both needed to be in Singapore in two months' time, we made a plan and jotted down a route – which had disappeared by the morning – and a few weeks later we were the proud owners of two identical, bright-yellow bicycles. Rucksacks were sent home and we squeezed all our essentials into two small panniers.

I was ready for an adventure. In soaring heat and 100 per cent humidity we cycled down the east coast of Malaysia, with the aid of a cheap road atlas and a guidebook. Accommodation was sparse so our journey was planned around the scattering of hostels and hotels down the coast. From the beginning Marianna and I got along and we remain great friends to this day. Some days we woke up and decided we couldn't get on the bikes so we would sit and chill, or head over to the Perhentian Islands or Tioman Island for a few days of swimming and snorkelling. En route, the locals greeted us with a mixture of incredulity and horror – two women cycling unaccompanied was a rare sight then, especially in some of the smaller villages – but when we stopped they would rush over and offer us drinks and food and then dispatch us with a cheery wave. We arrived in Singapore a few weeks later with bodies and bikes intact and a huge sense of achievement.

After a few days in Singapore, Marianna flew home with her bike and Meena arrived from London. Her news from home could have been from a different universe. Over the last few months I had travelled through India, Thailand and Laos, met many special people, encountered different sights, smells and food and had endless new experiences. Home seemed a long way away.

Of course, travelling is not always easy. There were lonely times, frustrations and some very bad days. I remember lying on a flea-ridden bed in India with a stomach bug, convinced I was going to die. On bad days I thought about flying home. But the bad days always seemed to be followed by a good day: a beautiful sight, a conversation or a meeting, something to make me change my mind.

Meena and I chatted into the night. It wasn't until the next morning that she pulled a buff-coloured envelope out of her bag and handed it to me saying, 'I'm afraid I have some papers that need signing.'

I took the envelope and stuffed it into the bottom of my rucksack.

Sally Watts works as a part-time practice nurse in London, and over the years has combined nursing with her passion for travel. Highlights include a six-month overland trip across Africa, working as a medic in Guyana for the youth development organisation Raleigh International and working with birth attendants in remote villages in Madagascar. Wherever she goes she writes a travel journal and considers this an essential travel item. She lives in London with her partner Monty, and Matilda the campervan lives outside.

Tips

One of the best parts of travelling by yourself is that you can do whatever you want. Make the most of it. *Anna Finch*

Make an effort with the local language. Sounds obvious, but it really does open hearts and doors. Even learning 'hello' and 'thank you' helps a great deal, and communication is a sure fire way to make a lone traveller feel less lonely. Trying at a language can cause great mirth too, which is always a good thing. *Claire Morsman*

Don't feel that you've got to enjoy every minute. Some days can be tough, boring, frustrating and/or upsetting, just as they can at home, so grit your teeth and hope tomorrow will be better. Disasters, once recovered from, often become treasured and entertaining memories. *Janice Booth*

Bring a journal. Without anyone to share your travel experiences with, some memories may disappear forever, so record things. Solo travel gives you space and time to observe everything going on around you. And as the trip goes on, you can look back at the early pages and notice how your confidence has grown. *Vicki Brown*